MW01591194

© Copyright 2015

Disclaimer

The information provided in this book is designed or written to
provide helpful information on the subjects discussed. The author's
books are only meant to provide the reader with the basic knowledge
of a certain topics related to different subjects, without any
warranties whether the student will, or will not, be able to
incorporate and apply all the information provided. Although the
writer has made his best effort to share the insights of JSON with the
help different tutorials in this book but there is need to understand
that learning is a difficult task and each person needs a different
timeframe to fully incorporate a new topic. Neither this book nor any
other book of the writer promises that reader will learn certain topics
and subjects at any extent within a certain timeframe. This is all
because learning is process that depends various aspects including
the learner's capability to understand, practice and perform the topic
or subject he/she is learning.

LEARN JSON IN A DAY

DAY

The Ultimate Crash Course to Learning the Basics of JSON in No Time

Table of Contents

Chapter 1: Introduction to JSON

Objective: This chapter introduces you to JSON, helps you understand why it's used, and how it's used in the development industry.

For many years, XML was the standard format for structured data. It was easy to use and similar to HTML with tags that contained data. XML was the popular format for data being passed between APIs or even database output and input.

Then, JavaScript Object Notation (JSON) was introduced at the beginning of the millennium. In 2005, Yahoo began offering JSON as an output data type, and it quickly became a de facto for data transfers. What makes JSON an interesting option is that it's completely platform and language independent. You can use JSON in older systems such as Classic ASP and Java or newer languages such as C#, Ruby, and PHP. The data content is text-based, so it's easily read across all platforms, and even humans can read and understand a JSON file's content.

XML is still used in some applications, but JSON is quickly overtaking the older format as the standard API communication tool. JSON also works well with Ajax and jQuery, so you can send and receive asynchronous communications. Asynchronous communication is more user friendly and reduces load on the web server. Instead of refreshing the entire web page, you can code your site to send and receive JSON communication with one HTTP request.

Why Use JSON?

You might ask yourself why you should change to JSON from XML if XML works just fine. The problem with XML is that it's an extremely bulky and has a lot of overhead to use it. Tags, properties and other bulky data were included in an XML file. For a small data set, the overhead was huge. As a matter of fact, most programmers were unimpressed with XML when it was first introduced. It was difficult to read and difficult to parse through. As it turns out, JSON was a much better option and programmers' first reactions were accurate.

JSON is much simpler, has little overhead to use, and it has a format that is easy to read. For instance, if you have an object with a first and last name, you can easily identify what components in the JSON output matches with this input.

There are no properties are markup in JSON, which also makes it much more lightweight. With XML, properties and markup determined a file's syntax structure. Any missing tag could throw off any XML parser. JSON also requires proper structure, but it's much easier to implement and create.

If you've ever developed with XML, you know that you must build a document piece by piece, and any small structural error throws off your document. It could be easy to identify the issue with smaller documents, but larger XML documents are difficult to troubleshoot. With JSON, you get a textual representation of your data without the bulky tags and markup.

JSON is also universal, so you can use JSON with any language or platform. Since it's text based, JSON uses Unicode. This means that an application written for a Spanish audience by an English developer can use JSON without any special internationalization on the code.

Tags don't need to be in any specific language – the coder just needs to identify each object item. The value can be in any language.

Overall, JSON is widely becoming the standard for data driven applications. There are numerous libraries that handle parsing of the data, so you don't even need much experience with JSON to get started. With just a small amount of understanding, you can work with JSON data without much work on your part. Several libraries handle building JSON objects as well. For instance, passing data to and from a C# controller can be done in one line of code using a specific .NET framework library.

Finally, another great benefit to JSON is that you don't need any special software to work with it. Remember, it's a text based format, so you don't need any software to build objects or even read JSON files. Some development environments help you view JSON files by color coding variables and objects. Color coding helps developers better read the content just like it helps them code more easily.

In this eBook, we will show you how to use JSON, and you'll see that many of these benefits are illustrated with the code and structure. Once you work with JSON, you'll never want to return to XML again.

What is JSON Used For?

For the most part, JSON is used in JavaScript since it's a JavaScript object. You can still pass JSON in other languages, but most people use JSON for asynchronous transactions. You'll see a lot of JSON in Ajax and jQuery code. The Ajax or jQuery code passes information asynchronously to the main language such as C# or PHP.

We should note what "asynchronous" calls mean to a coder and a user. Traditionally, when a user sent data to a web application, the user clicked a "Submit" button and the browser would send the information to the web server. Once the data was processed, a response is sent back to the user's browser and a new page is displayed. All elements of the new web page were retrieved and re-rendered on the user's browser including navigation, sidebars, footers and any common content. This was sufficient for older web applications, but users have become more demanding and want faster web responses.

Asynchronous web calls solve the issue of speed and fast responses. Asynchronous web calls only send the form portion of a web page back to the web server. The footer, header, sidebars and any other static components on the page aren't sent to the server. The result? A faster response and users don't have to wait for a response. The transaction is faster for the server because it doesn't need to retrieve and process all objects on a web page. It only needs to process the data, which is usually processed on a database. The small amount of processing power needed from the web server leaves resources for other more intensive applications. The result is a better experience for the user. The benefit is less processing power needed from the web server, which results in a cost savings and efficiency for website owners.

Now that you understand asynchronous versus synchronous calls to a web server, you can understand the way JSON works and what it's used for. You've probably come across JSON calls on several websites and don't even realize it.

First, JSON is used to pass data back and forth in a web application.

This web application could be an internal application used for a corporate environment, or it could be a public website. Let's take an example of signing in to an application.

First, you open the page and see a login prompt. When you type your username and password into the text boxes, you then click "Submit." The submit button is disabled and you see a spinning "Wait" prompt in your browser. Chances are that the application is passing your username and password using JSON formatted input using Ajax. Of course, when you pass a username and password to a web application, it should be encrypted. Encryption is handled by the web server's SSL or TLS certificate. When you pass private data between your browser and a web application, always make sure HTTPS is in the address bar.

After the database checks for your username and password, it either sends bad a "Yes" or a "No" (generally speaking) to the web application to let it know if the credentials entered are correct. If they are correct, usually data sent back includes some information about your account including your account ID and possibly your first and last name. The information is then displayed in your web browser. This back and forth information is formatted in JSON. The information is packaged as a JSON object with your account ID, first name, and last name as a variable and the information that matches your account as values.

JSON is also used in APIs. Application Programming Interfaces (APIs) are programs that run on a web server to send data back and forth in a specific format. APIs are generally used when you want other programmers to work with your data. For instance, Twitter has an API. You can query it to get Twitter data. The data sets vary as you can query any type of Twitter data including tweets, shares, tweet content and accounts.

All of this can be done using any language, because Twitter sends data back in JSON format. Since JSON is a universal format, whatever language you use to program your local application is irrelevant. The language Twitter uses to process your queries is also irrelevant. The language used isn't important because the data passed back and forth is in the JSON format.

Web form posts and APIs are just two reasons you would want to learn and use JSON. It's an inexpensive language in terms of resources and format, and it is easy to work with.

Pros and Cons of JSON

As with any language on the Internet, JSON has its pros and cons. The pros definitely outweigh the cons, but you should still know the disadvantages before you start learning and using the language in your application.

We mentioned several advantages in the first section. JSON is a universal language, it's text based, it has no complicated tags and markup, and it doesn't require the programmer to understand a complicated architecture. The architecture is a simple variable-value pair that is contained within a JSON object.

You don't need a special JSON creator to build a JSON file. You can build a JSON file by typing it in a text editor, although it isn't recommended. The syntax is easy to read and write, but it can get complicated when you have large data sets. Most language frameworks have a library that works directly with JSON, so you don't need to manually parse the data set. This is much easier than building your own format. You could build your own data format, but then you'd need to create your own library, build your own parser, and then troubleshoot and debug the application.

This is much more cumbersome and time-consuming than just using the standard JSON libraries provided to you.

One thing to note when comparing JSON to XML is that JSON is a data driven format. XML is a document driven format. XML brings with it much more information within the document, which can still be useful in some ways. For instance, you might want to make one record red. You could set that property in the XML document, so your web page knows to format the entry with red font. With JSON, you don't have that option. There are no properties or methods for handling data. You just get data and the web application must know how to handle the information, format it, and assign properties to it.

Another disadvantage is that JSON is only for flat data. Meaning, it only holds and transmits strings, numbers, and other standard values. You can't transfer any media types such as audio and video. It's not meant for any binary information, so you can't transfer images or executables. All of these formats must be dealt with in other forms in your application.

JSON is also lightweight, so you don't use much overhead when you transfer data even if the data set contains thousands of records. Remember when we mentioned APIs? APIs are capable of transferring huge amounts of data. For the most part, you want to limit the amount of data you transfer even if you have large amounts of bandwidth for your application. Large data sets slow down your application and eat up your bandwidth. Most hosting companies charge extra monthly fees when you go over your allotted bandwidth amounts. It's also costly for computer resources to process large amounts of data.

With XML, if you transfer large data sets, you'd most certainly cause issues with bandwidth and resources. With JSON, you still want to be aware of the amount of data you're transferring, but it lets you transfer larger data sets than with standard XML without the huge overhead to your systems.

If you need to work with other programmers, JSON is widely understood, so you should stick with a standard. Making your own standard creates confusion within the programming community. When you want programmers to use your API, it's best to give them a format that they can easily work with. It promotes usage for your application, and it makes it easier for everyone to get to know your application.

You will still come across XML in the field. It's still a viable option for transferring data, but you should know JSON as well. As a matter of fact, XML is slowly becoming obsolete in the industry. One reason it is still available is that legacy systems still use the format for its APIs and data transfers. It's difficult to change your platform syntax when it's engrained into your system. As you get more familiar with JSON, you will learn to appreciate its value and benefits.

Lab Questions

1. What is one reason why you would use JSON instead of XML when building an API?

a. JSON holds more data than a standard XML document
b. JSON is easier to transfer than XML information
c. JSON is lightweight and uses less bandwidth
d. XML is no longer used

Explanation: JSON doesn't have the tags, properties and other heavy information needed to format a document like an XML transfer.

2. What is the basic format for JSON documents?

a. value-variable
b. variable-value
c. tag-value
d. tag-variable

Explanation: a JSON file contains a list of variable-value pairs that make up the JSON object.

3. What is one disadvantage of using JSON for your API?

a. You can't use string variables
b. You can't use numbers for data
c. You can't have more than 100 records
d. You can't transfer media information

Explanation: JSON is for plain data only, so you cannot use it to transfer video, audio, images or any other binary information.

4. What is an advantage of using JSON in your applications?

a. It's lightweight and uses less bandwidth
b. It's lets you use output properties such as color formats
c. You can attach other media with JSON objects
d. JSON is parsed faster than XML

Explanation: Because JSON does not have the bulky tags and document standards of XML, its lightweight features save companies money for bandwidth and server overhead.

5. Can you store a JSON file in an external document? (T/F)

True

Explanation: you can store JSON information in an external file with the .json file extension.

6. What does the term JSON stand for?

a. Java Script Object Network
b. JavaScript Object Notation
c. JavaScript Open Notation
d. JavaScript Object Networking

Chapter 2: Basic Syntax

Objective: This chapter focuses on basic JSON syntax, so you can learn to recognize, read and create JSON objects.

Just like any other language, JSON has a specific syntax. Although it's easy to write JSON and read its data, any minor mistake can make your JSON file unreadable. However, before you know what you need to format the syntax, you need to know basic syntax. Knowing the syntax can also help you troubleshoot any issues when you run across errors in your code.

Basic JSON Structure

If you remember from chapter 1, we described the basic JSON syntax as a variable-value pair. If you've ever worked with any other languages, you'll probably recognize the key-value pair for some structures. JSON uses the similar syntax, making it easy to recognize data format and information.

Let's take a look at a basic variable-value pair.

"FirstName" : "John"

That's it! That is the variable-value pair you'll see throughout an entire JSON file. However, this is just one pair, and you probably want to use more than one when you set up a JSON file. Here is an example of multiple value pairs.

"FirstName" : "John", "FirstName" : "Jane", "FirstName" : "Joan"

As you can see from the above data, we have three values. Although the same variable name is used, we have three different values. You must always specify the variable name when you work with JSON data even if it's the same variable name throughout the entire file.

After each variable name is a colon. This is also standard and must be used to separate the variable names from the values. It indicates to the JSON engine that the variable name has ended and the next string or number is the actual value.

Next is the actual value. This is the meat of any application, because it's dynamic and what you've queried the application for. You want to know the names of users in the system, and this data set gives you three users with their first names.

Finally, notice the comma in between each pair. This is also an imperative part of the JSON data structure. A comma separates the variable-value pairs. Any JSON file with two or more pairs has at least one comma. Whether it's 2 or 1000 records, each record must be separated with a comma.

This is the basic structure for any JSON input, output or statically stored file.

We showed you string values, but JSON also lets you use numbers. You can use either integers or decimal point numbers. Integers are numbers without any decimal values. Floats or decimal numbers have decimal precision. It's important to make this distinction in your code or your applications can either throw an error or have bugs.

A JSON variable-value pair with integers or decimal numbers don't use quotes around the values. The variable names still require quotes, but you don't need them around a number value.

For anyone who has worked with any other types of languages, you'll recognize this type of syntax structure. It's standard across any language.

Let's take a look at a variable-value JSON pair with numbers.

"AccountNumber" : 1001, "AccountNumber" : 1002, "AccountNumber" : 1003

The above JSON values are a list of account numbers. As you can see, the variable name is still in quotes. The values are numeric, so they do not have any quotes. This tells the JSON engine that you intend to use numbers for the values. You could put quotes around these numbers, but they would be interpreted as strings. While this isn't technically incorrect, you don't want to use strings when you can use numeric values. When you use numbers as strings, you must first convert the string to a number format, and then you can calculate your results. This can not only add extra overhead in your programs, but it can also get confusing when another programmer must be able to read your code. You want to streamline your code as much as possible, and this is one of the standards in the programming world.

You can also use true and false values and even arrays. We'll show you arrays in the last part of this section. For now, let's take a look at true and false values.

"ActiveAccount" : true, "ActiveAccount" : false, "ActiveAccount" : true

In this example, we have a list of records that indicate if an account is active or not. You would, of course, mix this information with data that links an account number, but for this example we're just illustrating the way you can use the true and false values.

Notice that these values also don't use quotes. That's because true and false are actually one and zero in binary. One is equal to true and zero is equal to false. When you use the true or false Boolean values in any language, the operating system and compiler turns the values to one or zero no matter how these values are represented in code.

The final major construct in JSON is the array. If you've used any other form of programming, you should recognize an array. An array is one variable that contains several values. For instance, you might have a list of phone numbers for one customer. The phone numbers could represent a home and cell number. You return this list of numbers in an array for JSON to package and send to the application.

Let's take a look at how a list of phone numbers contained in an array would look like in JSON.

"PhoneNumbers" : ["555-555-5555", "666-666-6666", "777-777-7777"]

Pretty simple! The array pair still follows the same syntax rules as the other variable and value pairs, except this structure uses the open and close brackets to contain data. You could return three phone number variables, but this would make your code much less efficient. Instead, all three phone numbers are contained in the JSON array structure with each phone number separated by a comma.

You can also have multiple arrays. For instance, you probably have more than one phone number for more than one customer. You would return multiple arrays for each record. Let's take a look at an example.

"PhoneNumbers" : ["555-555-5555", "666-666-6666", "777-777-7777"], "PhoneNumbers" : ["444-444-4444", "333-333-3333", "222-222-2222"]

Notice that the syntax is actually the same as the other examples. We have two array phone number variables. Just like the active accounts example using true and false, you would also link this information with the user names and account IDs, but we're just showing an example of what multiple arrays look like in a JSON object. The multiple variables are also separated with a comma, but the arrays still use their own values within brackets.

One last type of value is null. A null value is used when you don't have any data in the value for your pair. Let's take a look at a list of values that would return a null.

"FirstName" : "John", "FirstName" : "Jane", "FirstName" :

Notice that the last pair has no value. JSON interprets this as a null value. Null does not indicate no value. Null values are values on their own, but they do indicate to the programmer that nothing was passed in the JSON pair.

JSON objects can also be passed within a parent object. Understanding JSON objects is in the next section, and we'll show you how to add them to your list of variable pairs.

Create a JSON Object

Now that you know how to create variable-name pairs in JSON, you need to use them in a JSON object. The pairs are not complete, valid JSON syntax. If you tried to send any of the above data in an application, it would tell you that the JSON format is not valid, because you don't have it in an object.

JSON objects are similar to JavaScript objects. First, let's take a look at a JavaScript object.

```
var user = { };
user.FirstName = "John";
user.LastName = "Smith";
```

The above JavaScript code creates an object named user. The user is then populated with a first and last name property. While this is viable for JavaScript, it doesn't account for transferring data back and forth between a web server and a user's browser.

Now let's take a look at how an object is created in JavaScript

```
{ "FirstName" : "John", "LastName" : "Smith" }
```

As you can see, JSON uses the open and closing brackets, but no object is assigned. That's because we don't need an object named yet. We let the processing language determine the object name. Remember that JSON only cares about data and formatting data. It does not care about the processing language whether it's C#, Ruby, PHP, or Java. This gives it the ability to be universal and a standard that isn't based on platform.

Now that you know how to work with a JavaScript object, let's look at an example of a JSON object that contains another object. For instance, let's go back to the phone number example. We used a list of numbers in an array, but we don't know which number belongs to which property. For instance, there is no way for us to distinguish the home number from the cell phone number. Let's change the way we use the output and use a phone number object instead. We'll add the phone number object to our existing "John Smith" user account object.

```
{
"FirstName" : "John", "LastName" : "Smith",
"PhoneNumbers" :
        {
                "type" : "Home",
                "number" : "333-333-3333"
        },
        {

                "type" : "Cell",
                "number" : "444-444-4444"

        }
}
```

The above structure is a little more complex. We still have the standard first and last name variables we used earlier. We have the opening and closing brackets for the main object, and then we see another opening and closing brackets. These secondary brackets also indicate an object, but it's an object within an object. Notice that the object is set after the "PhoneNumbers" variable. When you use these structures, the JSON engine then knows that the variable contains an object. The object is referred to with the variable name, so this object is referred to as the PhoneNumber object.

Since we have two phone numbers, each number is an object with a type and the actual number. You must use brackets for an object representation, and then use commas to separate each object just like when you separate other types of data.

HTML Example

Now that you know what a basic JSON object looks like, let's take a look at an actual HTML example. This helps you understand how to take the JSON object and use it in a real-world application.

First, let's create a basic shell HTML page. You can use any HTML editor and even a text editor. One good HTML editor is Notepad++. This application color codes numerous languages for easier coding. It also recognizes HTML and JSON formats, so it's a good way to code your basic HTML pages.

Open your favorite editor and copy and paste the following code.

```
<!DOCTYPE html>
<html>
<body>

<h2>JSON User Account Example</h2>

<p id="myuser"></p>

<script>

</script>

</body>
</html>
```

Since this ebook is on JSON and not HTML, we'll skip explaining the HTML structure. One thing you should know is that JavaScript is written in the script tags, so any JSON and JavaScript code should be within these two tags. You can also create external JavaScript and JSON files. JavaScript files have the .js file extension and JSON files have the .json file extension.

Now let's add some JSON and JavaScript code.

Let's first create the JSON object.

```
<!DOCTYPE html>
<html>
<body>

<h2>JSON User Account Example</h2>

<p id="myuser"></p>

<script>
var user = '{
"FirstName" : "John", "LastName" : "Smith",
"PhoneNumbers" :
        {
                "type" : "Home",
                "number" : "333-333-3333"
        },
        {
                "type" : "Cell",
                "number" : "444-444-4444"
        }
}';

</script>

</body>
</html>
```

Notice that the same structure is used, but we've turned the JSON object into a string and assigned it to a JavaScript variable named "user." The string is important, because JavaScript won't recognize the plain text values as a JSON object until we call a specific JSON function.

The next step is to parse the JSON into an object. You can use the JSON parse function to turn the string into an object. Let's add it to the code.

```html
<!DOCTYPE html>
<html>
<body>

<h2>JSON User Account Example</h2>

<p id="myuser"></p>

<script>
var user = '{
"FirstName" : "John", "LastName" : "Smith",
"PhoneNumbers" :
        {
                "type" : "Home",
                "number" : "333-333-3333"
        },
        {
                "type" : "Cell",
                "number" : "444-444-4444"
        }
}';
var jobject = JSON.parse(user);

</script>

</body>
</html>
```

The JSON string is now converted into an object and transferred to the jobject JavaScript object variable.

Finally, you probably want to display the object to your users. We set up a div object to display the JSON information. You can use the JavaScript innterHTML property to write data to your web page.

The following code is the final HTML file that performs a display of your JSON object.

```
<!DOCTYPE html>
<html>
<body>

<h2>JSON User Account Example</h2>

<p id="myuser"></p>

<script>
var user = '{
"FirstName" : "John", "LastName" : "Smith",
"PhoneNumbers" :
        {
                "type" : "Home",
                "number" : "333-333-3333"
        },
        {
                "type" : "Cell",
                "number" : "444-444-4444"
        }
}';
var jobject = JSON.parse(user);
document.getElementById("myuser").innterHTML =
jobject.FirstName

</script>

</body>
</html>
```

The above code takes the FirstName property from the object and displays it in the myuser div tag. That's all it takes to work with a JSON object.

Once the structure is created, you can use this shorthand to retrieve variable values and display them to your users.

Lab Questions

1. What is the basic format for a variable-value pair in JSON?

a. "variable" : "value"
b. "value" : "variable"
c. variable : value
d. variable ; value

Explanation: Both variable and value are in quotes when you use a string for a value. If you use numbers, you do not need to use quotes. The basic format is variable: value in JSON.

2. Write the JSON code that is an object containing data for a first and last name.

{ "FirstName" : "John", "LastName" : "Smith" }

Explanation: The open and closing brackets are the start and end for the object. Each variable-value pair is separated by commas.

3. Write the proper syntax for an array value in a JSON object.

"PhoneNumbers" : ["555-555-5555", "666-666-6666", "777-777-7777"]

Explanation: Array values have a variable name, but the values are contained within opening and closing brackets. Notice that array brackets are different than the opening and closing object brackets.

4. Write the JSON code that represents an object with a FirstName, LastName, and PhoneNumber variable. The PhoneNumber variable should be an object with two types "Cell" and "Home" phone numbers.

```
{
"FirstName" : "John", "LastName" : "Smith",
"PhoneNumbers" :
        {
                "type" : "Home",
                "number" : "333-333-3333"
        },
        {
                "type" : "Cell",
                "number" : "444-444-4444"
        }
}
```

Explanation: Objects within JSON objects also have opening and closing brackets with their own variable and values separated by a comma.

Chapter 3: JSON Arrays

Objective: JSON arrays use one variable name to contain several values. This chapter helps you understand arrays, create them, and parse their information.

We briefly covered JSON arrays in the previous chapter, but arrays are much more complex than regular values. It's important that you learn how to work with arrays and objects within objects. Even more complex is understanding arrays within other objects. As you can probably imagine, a JSON object can get pretty complex once you start working with numerous data sets. Although the information is easy to read, it can get complex to the point where you are unable to visually parse the information. This is why you should rely on programming language libraries to ensure that your data is properly parsed.

Understanding Arrays

Arrays can contain 1 or 1000 values. Arrays are larger variables that contain a list of values needed to process data. Let's look at a visual representation of an array variable.

VariableName = { 1, 2, 3 }

Notice that the variable name is defined just once, but the variables are contained within brackets. These brackets indicate that the variable will hold more than one value. This array contains three values.

Array values are assigned an index. Index values start with 0 in any computer language. You must remember this fact because looping through arrays cause errors if you attempt to retrieve data from an undefined index. With our VariableName variable, it contains 3 values, so the index numbers are defined as 3-1 or n-1. With our example, the VariableName array has indexes 0, 1, and 2. If you tried to retrieve data from index 3, your program would display an error.

It's important to remember that all array variables start with index 0. This is the main takeaway from this section. Arrays contain several values, but these values start with an index of 0. The index is incremented each time you add a new value to the array.

With JSON, you don't need to define the amount of indexes needed to contain the data. This is one advantage of JSON. For most languages, you must define the number of index positions when you create the variable. This is not necessary with JSON because the data set is built dynamically as you create the object.

Creating an Array

As you already know, arrays use opening and closing brackets. These brackets are different than the JSON object brackets. It's important to know the difference, because the JSON engine will improperly interpret data if it's represented incorrectly.

Let's first take a look at the properly created JSON array.

{ "CustomerOrders" : [100, 101, 102] }

In the last chapter, we used phone numbers as an example of an array, but there was no way to link those numbers to different types. For this reason, phone numbers are better left as JSON objects.

In this example, we use a CustomerOrders array. This array contains a list of customer order IDs. Each ID is a numeric value, so we don't need to contain them in quotes. We also have the necessary opening and close brackets, which are [and] characters.

We made the values a proper JSON object. The opening and close object brackets { and } are used to create the actual JSON object. In this example, the object only contains one variable. The CusotmerOrders variable is only one object that contains three values.

If you remember from our previous section explaining arrays, you should be able to identify the index numbers for each value. The first value – value 100 – is set at index 0. The second value – value 101 – is set at index 1. Finally, the third value – value 102 – is set at index 3. You'll need to know these index positions when you loop through the data or retrieve it in your JavaScript code.

Notice that each value is separated by a comma. Syntax is important in any programming language, and it's just as important in JSON. Remember to keep each value separate, or JSON could return an error or concatenate numeric values. When the language concatenates values incorrectly, this causes bugs in the system.

Arrays can also create null values in your code. For instance, if you forget to define a value in the array, the return value is null. This is usually a bug in the code, but it can be handled if you write efficient code.

The following example shows you a JSON array with a null value.

{ "CustomerOrders" : [100, 101,] }

Typically, the above code is an error. The ending comma should not be present, but you could make this mistake when you create the JSON object. The last value is null when you parse the data.

Finally, you should know how to create multiple arrays within a JSON object. Just like any other multiple variable object, you need to separate them using commas. The following is an example of a JSON object that contains two array variables.

{ "CustomerOrders" : [100, 101, 102], "CustomerOrders" : [200, 201, 202] }

The above JSON object contains two CustomerOrders arrays. These two arrays contain different order numbers. Typically, you'd use an object or identify the customer whose orders were contained in the arrays, but this gives you an example of how you would use multiple arrays in your JSON code.

Creating a JSON Array and Turning It Into an Object

Now that we know what a JSON array looks like and how we structure its data, we need to understand how to work with them in a JavaScript function. For the most part, you'll use JSON with JavaScript. Most applications combine the two languages to create the asynchronous calls to and from the application web server.

We'll use the same object as we had before. We'll use a CustomerOrder array and turn it into a full customer JSON object. First, let's set up a JSON object that contains a customer and the CustomerOrder array variable.

```
{
"FirstName" : "Joe",
"LastName" : "Smith",
"CustomerOrders" : [ 100, 101, 102 ]
 }
```

The above JSON object is a customer object. We have the first and last name of the customer, and then we use our CustomerOrders array that contains the customer's order IDs. Note that you could use another JSON object to specify customer orders. That's the beauty of programming. You can tackle different programming and structural design in several different ways. Some ways are more efficient than others, but you can generally design your JSON data structures in whatever way you feel is the best for your programming experience.

This structure works well when you don't need to know the number of customer orders or when you just want to use the indexes. Remember that three numeric values in the array mean that you have indexes n-1 or 0, 1, and 2 in this example.

What if we need to know more information with the order ID? We could create yet another array, but it's much more efficient to turn this array into an object. Let's do just that and turn our basic array into another JSON object.

```
{
"FirstName" : "Joe",
"LastName" : "Smith",
"CustomerOrders" : {
```

```
        { "type" : "Red", "OrderId" : 100 },
        { "type" : "Blue", "OrderId" : 101 },
        { "type" : "Green", "OrderId" : 102 }
}
```

You'll notice that we put much more information in the CustomerOrders variable, but this information makes it much easier to identify the information contained within the object. We changed the opening and closing brackets, which are important when you change an array to a JSON object. Remember that the parser needs correct syntax or you'll receive an error.

Each order is now an object of its own. We've added a type to the order information, so we can see the type of order that's created. We represent the order type as colors, but you can use any type of data to describe your orders. Now, instead of just seeing several numbers in an array, we have an OrderId variable that tells us the numbers are the customer's order ID. This customer has three orders.

As with any other values, we also separate our object variables with commas. If you forget the comma, the JSON engine will return an error. If you accidentally add an extra comma to the end of the last order object, you create a fourth order but the information is null. Keep track of your commas and brackets when working in JSON.

With this information, you can now more easily parse this data in JavaScript. In the next section, we'll give you a fully functional JavaScript and HTML example. However, let's take a quick look at when a JavaScript call to a JSON object looks like.

Let's assume we give this object the name of "user." You can retrieve the data in an intuitive way in JavaScript. Suppose we want to get the first order record for the user. The following JavaScript code retrieves the data.

user.CustomerOrders[1].OrderId

Notice the array index indicated in the JavaScript user variable. Remember that array indexes start with 0, so this representation gets the second value in the CustomerOrders object array.

With this basic syntax, let's turn what we know of JSON, arrays and objects and turn it into a more real-world problem in an HTML page.

HTML Real World Example: Using JSON Arrays in JavaScript

Just like the last chapter, it helps to give you a better idea of how to use JSON in a real world example. Since JSON is typically used in HTML pages with JavaScript, we're using HTML and script tags again. We first need to set up the basic HTML page template. We'll use the same template as the last chapter.

Open your HTML editor and copy and paste the following code into it.

```
<!DOCTYPE html>
<html>
<body>

<h2>JSON User Account Example</h2>

<p id="myuser"></p>

<script>

</script>

</body>
</html>
```

Remember that all JavaScript is placed within the script tags, so you must place all the JavaScript we're about to use within these tags. Let's add a JavaScript string variable that we'll then turn into an object.

Take a look at the following code.

```
<!DOCTYPE html>
<html>
<body>

<h2>JSON User Account Example</h2>

<p id="myuser"></p>

<script>
var user = '{
"FirstName" : "Joe",
"LastName" : "Smith",
"CustomerOrders" : {
        { "type" : "Red", "OrderId" : 100 },
        { "type" : "Blue", "OrderId" : 101 },
```

```
        { "type" : "Green", "OrderId" : 102 }
};
```

```
</script>
```

```
</body>
</html>
```

Remember that we first turn the JSON object into a string to add it to the JavaScript code. We gave the string name user, but we'll need a new object for the JSON object. Just like the last chapter, let's change the string to a JSON object.

```
<!DOCTYPE html>
<html>
<body>
```

```
<h2>JSON User Account Example</h2>
```

```
<p id="myuser"></p>
```

```
<script>
var user = '{
"FirstName" : "Joe",
"LastName" : "Smith",
"CustomerOrders" : {
        { "type" : "Red", "OrderId" : 100 },
        { "type" : "Blue", "OrderId" : 101 },
        { "type" : "Green", "OrderId" : 102 }
};
var jobject = JSON.parse(user);
```

```
</script>
```

```
</body>
</html>
```

The above changes to the code turns the user string into an object named jobject. We now have an object we can work with instead of using string values, which would be much more difficult to parse.

Now let's add some JavaScript variables that contain the user's first and last name, and the first order from our JSON CustomerOrders object.

```
<!DOCTYPE html>
<html>
<body>

<h2>JSON User Account Example</h2>

<p id="myuser"></p>

<script>
var user = '{
"FirstName" : "Joe",
"LastName" : "Smith",
"CustomerOrders" : {
        { "type" : "Red", "OrderId" : 100 },
        { "type" : "Blue", "OrderId" : 101 },
        { "type" : "Green", "OrderId" : 102 }
}';
var jobject = JSON.parse(user);
var firstname = jobject.FirstName;
var lastname = jobject.LastName
var firstorder = jobject.CustomerOrders[0].OrderId


</script>

</body>
```

Notice that we changed the index from the previous example to 0. We want the first order number, so we use index zero not 1. If we specified 1, we'd get the second order ID.

And finally, we probably want to display this information somewhere on the page. We have a paragraph tag named "myuser" that is meant to contain this data. We'll again use the innerHTML property to set the paragraph's information to the data we retrieved from the JSON object.

```
<!DOCTYPE html>
<html>
<body>

<h2>JSON User Account Example</h2>

<p id="myuser"></p>

<script>
var user = '{
"FirstName" : "Joe",
"LastName" : "Smith",
"CustomerOrders" : {
        { "type" : "Red", "OrderId" : 100 },
        { "type" : "Blue", "OrderId" : 101 },
        { "type" : "Green", "OrderId" : 102 }
}';
var jobject = JSON.parse(user);
var firstname = jobject.FirstName;
var lastname = jobject.LastName
var firstorder = jobject.CustomerOrders[0].OrderId
document.getElementById("myuser").innerHTML =
firstname + "<br>" + lastname + "<br>" +
        firstorder;
```

```
</script>

</body>
```

That's it! Note that we added the "<br>" HTML tags to the innerHTML string. This is to add carriage returns to the code. If we left them out, we'd get one big string of information with no spaces or breaks in between. As a matter of fact, the
 HTML tag stands for "break."

With this new information, you're now an expert at JSON arrays and turning those arrays into JSON objects for easier data structures. You also know how to parse those arrays, grab their data and display them on your HTML pages. We haven't covered data types, so that's the next section in our JSON journey.

Lab Questions

1. When you want to retrieve the first value in an array, what is the appropriate index number?

a. 0
b. 1
c. -1
d. null

Explanation: The first index value in any array in any language is always 0. It's important to remember to avoid retrieving null values in JSON.

2. Write the proper syntax to create a JSON array that contains three order IDs.

{ "CustomerOrders" : [100, 101, 102] }

Explanation: An array always gets a variable name and then opening and closing brackets. These brackets are different than brackets used for JSON objects. Values are separated by a comma.

3. Assume you have a variable named user that contains a JSON object. You want to retrieve the first value in the CustomerOrders array. Write the code that retrieves this value.

user.CustomerOrders[0]

Explanation: The CustomerOrders array name is used after the user object. The 0 index position returns the first value from the array's list of values.

4. If you recall, we turned the CustomerOrders array into a JSON object. Reconstruct this object using type and OrderId as the two object variables.

```
{
"FirstName" : "Joe",
"LastName" : "Smith",
"CustomerOrders" : {
        { "type" : "Red", "OrderId" : 100 },
        { "type" : "Blue", "OrderId" : 101 },
        { "type" : "Green", "OrderId" : 102 }
}
}
```

Explanation: This JSON object contains a customer's first and last name and three orders for the customer.

Chapter 4: JSON Data Types

Objective: Every program has its own data type structures. This chapter reviews the data types you can use in JSON objects.

Data types are the values you can store in an object. Every programming language uses specific data types. More advanced languages even let you create your own structures, but JSON is much simpler and only works with data. We've covered several data types but none in detail. JSON is not an advanced language, so you can only use basic types. If you've ever worked with any other languages, you'll recognize some of the data types.

The Main Data Types in JSON

You might hear developers call JSON data types "primitive types." Primitive types are the data values that are available in any language. The following data types are the basic, primitive types available in JSON.

Numbers -- decimal and integers
Strings – the text you see with any character, number or special character
Booleans – these values equal true or false. True and false are translated to one and zero respectively
Null – this is a special value that represents no value was given

These data types can easily translate between languages. For instance, a numeric value is universally known regardless of the language you use to calculate and process the information. This is another reason why the data types are referred to as primitive.

JSON has two more data types that are unique to the language. The following two data types are available in other languages but their structures are much different.

Object – a variable that contains a list of records
Array – a variable that contains several values

We'll discuss all of these data types in more detail in this chapter, and we'll show you how to use them.

Using JSON Data Types

We'll start with the easiest data type to understand – the number. In programming, it's important to know that there are subtypes for numerical variables. JSON only has two numeric values – a decimal and an integer value. Sometimes decimal numbers are referred to as a fraction.

Numbers

JSON also understands exponents. For instance, if you have a number of 1000, you can represent this number in shorthand. The following exponential value represents the value 1000.

10E+3

The above value translates to 10 to the third or 1000. This seems basic for a value of 1000, but think about values with 10 zeros. Shorthand makes it much easier to represent and store values. The following JSON object represents how a number is stored.

{ "FirstName" : "John", "LastOrderId" : 100 }

Notice that the string value is contained in quotes but the number OrderId variable uses a number with no quotes. This is a critical difference when programming in JSON. If you accidentally add quotes around a number, you'll need to convert the value to an integer before you can perform calculations on it.

String

Strings are the "words" in programming. They are always contained in quotes in any programming language including the JSON language. Strings can contain more than just numeric values. They can contain a number of characters along with special characters. There are also characters that represent certain actions such as backspace, form feed, new line, and horizontal tab.

Let's take a look at a JSON object with string variables.

{ "FirstName" : "John", "LastName" : "Smith" }

We used the same FirstName variable as we used in the previous section. We then added a LastName variable. Both of these variables are strings. You could identify a string for its "words" or characters, but the main way to identify a string is that it's encompassed in quotes. Even variable names are strings, which is why they are encompassed in quotes as well.

We mentioned special characters that perform actions. Let's take a look at a JSON object that uses one of these special characters.

{ "Name" : "John\tSmith"}

In the above object, the \t special character is shown. This is the horizontal tab character. When the browser renders the information, the first name is first displayed, a tab is set, and then the last name is shown. This is a beneficial way to structure your display and format it in a better way.

Boolean

Boolean data types are easy to remember. They are just true or false. Different languages represent these values. Some languages let you use true or false notation. Others use zero and one. Boolean values are bits. Bits are either one or zero, so they are the smallest variables to allocate in memory. Instead of using the term true or false, it's more efficient to use one or zero. You can use either one or zero or true and false in JSON, but most developers use the true and false notation. Let's take a look at a JSON object with a Boolean variable.

{ "FirstName" : "John", "LastOrderId" : 100, "OrderShipped" : false }

In the above example, we have a JSON variable with a customer's first name and last order Id. The third variable lets us know if the order has shipped. In this example, the answer is false. When your database or program processes this data, the false notation translates to 0 since 0 is false in computer's binary language.

Array

We covered arrays in the last chapter. Arrays are more advanced JSON structures, and they let you contain several values within one variable. Arrays should be turned into JSON objects to make them more efficient when you need to retrieve structured data. We can use the array we used in the previous chapter to illustrate arrays in JSON.

```
{
"FirstName" : "Joe",
"LastName" : "Smith",
"CustomerOrders" : {
        { "type" : "Red", "OrderId" : 100 },
        { "type" : "Blue", "OrderId" : 101 },
        { "type" : "Green", "OrderId" : 102 }
}
```

Notice that we turned the CustomerOrders variable into an array of objects. We have a list of objects that represent the orders. The array contains the type of the order and the order Id. This type of representation makes it much easier to retrieve the data instead of using index positions.

Let's take a look at a basic array without being turned into an object to give you an idea of what an array looks like without the transition.

```
{ "CustomerOrders" : [ 100, 101, 102 ] }
```

The above JSON object contains an array with three values. We know that they are customer orders from the variable name, but it's much less inefficient since we can't retrieve values based on distinct variable names.

Object

You should know JSON objects by now. We've been working with them since chapter 2. A JSON data set is an object itself, but you can also place objects within objects. Let's look again at the array object we used in the previous section.

```
{
"FirstName" : "Joe",
"LastName" : "Smith",
"CustomerOrders" : {
        { "type" : "Red", "OrderId" : 100 },
        { "type" : "Blue", "OrderId" : 101 },
        { "type" : "Green", "OrderId" : 102 }
}
```

You know that the opening and closing brackets are used to indicate that we've defined a JSON object. But then we have another set of brackets. You can have numerous objects within objects in JSON. In this example, we have a CustomerOrders variable that has an array of objects. These objects represent the customer's orders. Each object is contained within its own set of brackets. We know that the CustomerOrders should contain a list of orders, and in this example we assume that orders have two properties: a type and an order id. We have the type and order Id for three orders. We can use these variable names to retrieve and set information within our JSON object using JavaScript.

Null Values

Null values are special values in any language. They indicate that a value is missing. This is no exception in JSON where you can send data with no value to a data set. You can purposely set a null value for a variable, or you can set no value and JSON will parse it as a null.

Let's take a look at an example of a JSON object that contains a null value.

{ "CustomerOrders" : [100, 101,] }

In this example, the third value in the CustomerOrders array contains a null value since no value is present. It's not recommended to use this kind of syntax, because it can cause bugs in your code. Null values are automatically changed to 0 in some languages, so you could accidentally insert an unintended bug in calculations throughout your code. If there is no value for a specific record, it's better to indicate a numeric value for the array code. You can also use null values in strings, which is much more convenient and less likely to cause bugs in your code.

Retrieving and Displaying Data in HTML

Now that you know all of the data types used in JSON, it's time to take a look at a real world example. You need to retrieve the data from a JSON object in JavaScript.

Let's first choose the JSON object we want to use. We'll use the same object as we used in the last chapter, but let's add more variables to cover the different data types we learned in this chapter.

```
{
"FirstName" : "John", "LastName" : "Smith",
"OrderShipped" : false, "CustomerId" : 100,
"PhoneNumbers" :
        {
                "type" : "Home",
                "number" : "333-333-3333"
        },
        {
```

```
        "type" : "Cell",
        "number" : "444-444-4444"
    }
}
```

We added two more values to the original JSON object. We added the OrderShipped variable and set the value to false. Remember that false translates to zero in any computer language. Next, we added a CustomerId variable that contains a numeric value.

Now that we have the JSON object set up, it's time to set up the HTML template. Let's use the same template that we have from the previous chapters. Copy and paste the following HTML template to your favorite HTML and JavaScript editor.

```html
<!DOCTYPE html>
<html>
<body>

<h2>JSON User Account Example</h2>

<p id="myuser"></p>

<script>

</script>

</body>
</html>
```

Remember that all JavaScript code must be within the script tags. You can create an external JavaScript or JSON file, but using inline code within an HTML page is much easier to illustrate for these examples.

Just know that all of the JavaScript we use in these lessons can be copy and pasted to a text file and stored separately. You give a JavaScript file the .js file extension.

First, let's add the JSON object to the script tags.

```
<!DOCTYPE html>
<html>
<body>

<h2>JSON User Account Example</h2>

<p id="myuser"></p>

<script>
var user = ' {
"FirstName" : "John", "LastName" : "Smith",
"OrderShipped" : false, "CustomerId" : 100,
"PhoneNumbers" :
        {
                "type" : "Home",
                "number" : "333-333-3333"
        },
        {
                "type" : "Cell",
                "number" : "444-444-4444"
        }
}';


</script>

</body>
</html>
```

Now we need to again parse the user string to a JSON object, so we can retrieve values using JSON object properties instead of parsing a messy string.

```html
<!DOCTYPE html>
<html>
<body>

<h2>JSON User Account Example</h2>

<p id="myuser"></p>

<script>
var user = ' {
"FirstName" : "John", "LastName" : "Smith",
"OrderShipped" : false, "CustomerId" : 100,
"PhoneNumbers" :
        {
                "type" : "Home",
                "number" : "333-333-3333"
        },
        {
                "type" : "Cell",
                "number" : "444-444-4444"
        }
}';
var jobject = JSON.parse(user);

</script>

</body>
</html>
```

We have a lot of data contained within this JSON object. We probably don't need it all, but we want to retrieve certain parts of it.

We can use the JSON object variable names to retrieve data. Typically, you assign these values to a JavaScript variable.

Let's take a look at some code that retrieves the user's first and last name, the customer Id, and the first order information.

```
<!DOCTYPE html>
<html>
<body>

<h2>JSON User Account Example</h2>

<p id="myuser"></p>

<script>
var user = ' {
"FirstName" : "John", "LastName" : "Smith",
"OrderShipped" : false, "CustomerId" : 100,
"PhoneNumbers" :
        {
                "type" : "Home",
                "number" : "333-333-3333"
        },
        {
                "type" : "Cell",
                "number" : "444-444-4444"
        }
}';
var jobject = JSON.parse(user);
var firstname = jobject.FirstName;
var lastname = jobject.LastName
var firstorder = jobject.CustomerOrders[0].OrderId
```

```
</script>

</body>
</html>
```

Notice how we retrieved the data. We use the jobject object variable. This variable was named when we converted the user string to a JSON object. Because the string is now an object, we can use the object's variable names.

One issue that you can run into is if the string isn't formatted properly. A string that isn't formatted properly won't parse properly, and it can cause an error in your programming. Always ensure that your JSON string is structured properly.

With our variables created, we can now display the information to our user. We use the HTML elements to display data. JavaScript integrates well with HTML, so we can use the JavaScript innerHTML property on the HTML document to display to the user. Let's take a look at the complete code.

```
<!DOCTYPE html>
<html>
<body>

<h2>JSON User Account Example</h2>

<p id="myuser"></p>

<script>
var user = ' {
"FirstName" : "John", "LastName" : "Smith",
"OrderShipped" : false, "CustomerId" : 100,
"PhoneNumbers" :
     {
```

```
                    "type" : "Home",
                    "number" : "333-333-3333"
            },
            {
                    "type" : "Cell",
                    "number" : "444-444-4444"
            }
    }';
var jobject = JSON.parse(user);
var firstname = jobject.FirstName;
var lastname = jobject.LastName
var firstorder = jobject.CustomerOrders[0].OrderId
document.getElementById("myuser").innerHTML =
firstname + "<br>" + lastname + "<br>" +
    firstorder;


</script>

</body>
</html>
```

This code displays the customer information in the paragraph tag we set up named "myuser." You can display this information in any HTML tag on the page. That's one of the benefits of using JavaScript in your code.

Now that you know JSON data types, you know the type of information you can send and retrieve in your applications. Any errors in your format can cause bugs, so ensure that you format your JSON strings accordingly.

Lab Questions

1. If you want to display a value of 10000 in scientific notation, what is the proper syntax?

a. 10E+3
b. 10E+4
c. 100+3
d. 1E+5

Explanation: The JSON language understands scientific notation, so you can use it to display numbers with several zeros without using as many resources as the full notation.

2. What is the proper notation for placing a horizontal tab within a string value?

a. { "Name" : "John\tSmith"}
b. { "Name" : "John\tabSmith"}
c. { "Name" : "JohntabSmith"}
d. { "Name" : "John Smith"}

Explanation: the \t special character indicates that you want to add a tab to the output format in your application.

3. When you don't include a value for a variable, what data type is used to represent the missing value?

a. 0
b. –
c. An empty string
d. Null

Explanation: A null value is a special data type that represents no value assigned to a JSON variable.

4. Write the proper JSON syntax for an object with an OrderId variable and a value of 100.

{ "OrderId" : 100 }

<u>Explanation:</u> Variable names are used in quotes, but numeric values are not encompassed in quotes.

Chapter 5: Making HTTP Requests

Objective: You often need to retrieve data from a web page, an API or a file on a web server. This chapter shows you how to make requests and read web pages using HTTP requests.

Up until now, we've used static JSON objects we've created within our HTML pages. This works in some environments, but you'll mostly need to retrieve data from another web page and process it within your JavaScript. The data is formatted in JSON, but you still need JavaScript to process it. These pages could be on your local server, within an API response or it could be a page on an external server. As long as you're able to retrieve the file, you can make a call to the web server, parse the file data, retrieve the JSON objects, and display the information to your users. You'll run into this type of programming often when you use APIs from different companies.

What is an HTTP Request?

HTTP requests are typically made by browsers, but you can create these requests on your own web pages. You use HTTP requests to make a request to a web server, retrieve data and use it to process data on your own server. These requests are not unlike what you make in a browser.

When you type a URL into your browser, the first thing the browser does is perform a DNS lookup.

Domain name service (DNS) servers check with a large database of domains to find the domain's IP address. The friendly name you type in the browser is just there for you to remember. The Internet doesn't work with friendly names. It works with IP addresses, which are the addresses of the Internet world.

Once the domain name server sends back an IP address, the browser can then make a connection with the web server that hosts the particular domain name website you typed into it originally. When the browser sends a request to the web server, it is an HTTP requests. These requests use the HTTP (Hypertext Transport Protocol) protocol. The HTTP protocol is the communication rules for the Internet and web browsing.

When the browser makes a request to the web server, it first requests that the server sends it information. The server sends an acknowledgement to the browser, and then the browser sends another response that requests the information or web page from the server. In some cases the page doesn't exist, so the server returns a 404 error with the 404 page. If the server is down for temporary maintenance, the server returns a 503 error message and returns a 503 error page. In other cases, the return message is a 301 redirect that then tells the browser that it's being forwarded to another domain and web server. When this happens, the process starts all over again.

In JavaScript, you can also send data with the HTTP request object. You'll use send and request commands to retrieve data from your HTML files, which contain script tags for JavaScript code. We'll again work with static HTML pages, but you can always place any JavaScript code in a separate js file and the JSON data can be located in a text file that usually has the .json file extension.

Retrieving Data from a URL

Before you begin experimenting with HTTP requests in your files, you need to set up an HTML template. We'll use the same template that we've used in previous chapters. Copy and paste the following code to your favorite HTML and JavaScript editor.

```
<!DOCTYPE html>
<html>
<body>

<h2>JSON User Account Example</h2>

<p id="myuser"></p>

<script>

</script>

</body>
</html>
```

Remember that any JavaScript code must be place within the script tag, and this example is no different. All of your JSON and JavaScript code should be placed within the script tags that we've set up in our HTML page.

The first line of code for any JavaScript HTTP request is using the XMLHttpRequest object. This object is a library that contains several methods that you can use to retrieve data from an external file. You must assign the object a variable just like you do when you create a JSON object.

You might notice that the object uses the prefix XML. This prefix was because the original object was used primarily for XML, but it is indeed useful for JSON requests as well.

Let's add the object to the HTML page template.

```
<!DOCTYPE html>
<html>
<body>

<h2>JSON User Account Example</h2>

<p id="myuser"></p>

<script>
var xmlhttp = new XMLHttpRequest();
var url = "myjson.json";
</script>

</body>
</html>
```

We added two lines of code within our template. The first one is the XMLHttpRequest object we mentioned earlier. We call the object and assign it a variable named xmlhttp.

The second line of code is a simple string. We name it URL because we need to know where to make the request to retrieve the JSON file. In this example, we're using a file that is local to our web server. This string value could be much more detailed with a domain name or an API URL where you retrieve the information.

Before we can retrieve the file, we first need to ensure that the status returned from the server is a status code of 200. A server status of 200 means that the server does not have any errors, it's not out of order for maintenance, and that no coding or hardware issues were found when the web page was processed.

We can create a function and add it to our code to check for any server errors. If the server returns the proper status code, only then will we continue to parse and process the JSON data.

Let's add the function to our JavaScript code.

```html
<!DOCTYPE html>
<html>
<body>

<h2>JSON User Account Example</h2>

<p id="myuser"></p>

<script>
var xmlhttp = new XMLHttpRequest();
var url = "myjson.json";
xmlhttp.onreadystatechange = function() {
    if (xmlhttp.readyState == 4 && xmlhttp.status == 200) {
        var user =
JSON.parse(xmlhttp.responseText);
        myFunction(user);
    }
}
</script>

</body>
</html>
```

We added quite a few lines of code to our JavaScript code. We added a function that you might not recognize. This function is actually an event function. An event function overrides default behavior and performs a custom action based on what you specify in the function code. In this example, we are overriding the "onreadystatechange" event.

This event is triggered when the HTTP request is ready to handle requests. Remember when we discussed the way a browser requests a web page? You don't actually retrieve the page until the web server acknowledges your request, and this request doesn't happen until a few lookups and requests are made to verify the server's IP. This is the same type of event. This event ensures that the web server is ready to receive the request for the JSON information before the request is actually made. In other words, this event function might not run for a few seconds after the XMLHttpRequest object is created.

In the above event function, after we verify that the server's status is 200 (which means OK in server language), it will then grab the response text from the request. We haven't added the request, so let's add that first before we explain further.

```
<!DOCTYPE html>
<html>
<body>

<h2>JSON User Account Example</h2>

<p id="myuser"></p>

<script>
var xmlhttp = new XMLHttpRequest();
var url = "myjson.json";
xmlhttp.onreadystatechange = function() {
    if (xmlhttp.readyState == 4 && xmlhttp.status
== 200) {
        var user =
JSON.parse(xmlhttp.responseText);
        myFunction(user);
    }
}
```

```
xmlhttp.open("GET", url, true);
xmlhttp.send();
</script>

</body>
</html>
```

Now we added the actual request. We used the HTTP request "open" method to initialize the request. This method is a part of the XMLHttpRequest object we initialized earlier. Since we initialized it to the xmlhttp variable, we use this variable to call the open method.

Notice that the open method takes three parameters. The first parameter is a string named "GET." This tells the server to send the data using a GET method, which means that parameters and values are sent in querysting format. Query string format occurs when the variables and values are appended to a URL. The URL contains a question mark with key-value pairs. The following is an example of a URL with query string values appended.

Mydomain.com/page.php?firstname=john&lastname=smith

Notice that the query string starts after the question mark, and each variable is separated by the ampersand (&) character. Key-value parks are connected using the equal sign.

The next parameter is the URL variable. We already set this variable in the second line of code that says the URL is set to myjson.json. We assume this file contains JSON. You can use checks and balances to ensure that the code is JSON and that its syntax is viable, but error checking can get complicated, so we will skip this component to keep the code clean and easy to understand.

The final parameter is set to "true." Remember in the last chapter we discussed Boolean values, which can be either true or false. In this example, we use true. Also remember that true translates to 1 in computer binary language.

The reason for this parameter is that you want to set the transaction to asynchronous. When you use the true parameter in the open method, it tells the JavaScript code to send the request asynchronously. When you run this code asynchronously, the browser does not refresh the page, so the request is completely made in the background without the user's knowledge.

The final line of code that we added is the send method. This method takes no parameters, and it's used to actually send the request to the web server. We don't actually send the request until the send method is called. It might seem like the open statement sends the request, but it packages the request and waits for the send method. When the send method is triggered, the even function we created overrides any more requests until the status 200 is returned from the server. This helps avoid any issues when the server takes too long to process the information. When this happens, you could call other JavaScript methods and attempt to process the JSON data before the data is actually fully downloaded, which would cause errors in your applications.

Now we can return to the event function we created. It retrieves the data from the HTTP request and parses it. It then assigns the JSON object to the variable named user. We then call a function named "myFunction." This function sends the user parameter. We haven't defined or set up the myFunction function yet, so you will have an error if you try to run this code. It isn't complete.

Let's add the function to our code.

```html
<!DOCTYPE html>
<html>
<body>

<h2>JSON User Account Example</h2>

<p id="myuser"></p>

<script>
var xmlhttp = new XMLHttpRequest();
var url = "myjson.json";
xmlhttp.onreadystatechange = function() {
    if (xmlhttp.readyState == 4 && xmlhttp.status
== 200) {
        var user =
JSON.parse(xmlhttp.responseText);
        myFunction(user);
    }
}
xmlhttp.open("GET", url, true);
xmlhttp.send();
function myFunction(arr) {
    var out = "";
    var i;
    for(i = 0; i < arr.length; i++) {
        out += '<a href="' + arr[i].url + '">' +
        arr[i].display + '</a><br>';
    }
    document.getElementById("myuser").innerHTML =
out;
}
</script>

</body>
</html>
```

We just added a lot more code to the process. In this new code, we have a loop that iterates through the JSON code. What's great about this code is that it doesn't matter what type of data is contained in the file. In this example, though, we assume that the contained data is a list of URLs. However, you can use the code to display any number of records and any type of data.

We use the same paragraph we used in previous chapters to display the data. We use "myuser" to contain the parsed JSON information.

In the loop, we identify the number of records. With the number of records, we then use it to iterate through each record in the JSON file. For each record, we use the array index position to grab the data and then store it in an "out" variable. The out variable contains all of the JSON strings retrieved from the file. Once all records are iterated through and data is retrieved, we then display the output to the user. This process looks complex, but it happens within seconds. The time it takes to iterate through all records depends on the amount of records you contain in the file. Remember to keep JSON records to a minimum to increase performance. Iterating through a few hundred records won't harm your server's performance, but when you iterate through thousands and tens of thousands, it can cause an issue with server memory, CPU and bandwidth that can harm your website speed.

The code seems simple, but it can get much more complex when you have several fields to parse and display in the browser. For the most part, JSON information is very few records when you're working with client data. When you work with applications that send several thousands of records, it can be much more complex, but these applications are usually reserved for internal systems.

Knowing how to work with JSON files and data sent from an API or separate URL is an integral part of learning JSON. JSON is mostly used in API applications, so you'll run into HTTP requests several times in your programming career whether you're a junior level, intermediate level, or even senior level programmer.

Lab Questions

1. When you want to create an HTTP request from your JavaScript code, what is the object you use to initialize the variable?

a. XMLHttpRequest()
b. XMLHttp()
c. HttpRequest()
d. JsonRequest()

Explanation: The XMLHttpRequest object seems like it only retrieves XML data, but it also can be used to retrieve JSON data. It was named when XML was the original standard for data transfer.

2. What is the event you must override to ensure that you only send an HTTP request when the server is ready and the file exists on the server?

a. serverready
b. xmlready
c. serverstate
d. onreadystatechange

Explanation: The onreadystatechange detects when the server is ready to retrieve data and ensures that you don't try to parse JSON data before you actually retrieve the file.

3. What XMLHttpRequest method do you use to set up the URL and request type before you send the message?

a. retrieve
b. send
c. open
d. get

Explanation: The open method sets up the request but it doesn't actually send the request to the web server. You also set whether or not you want to send the request asynchronously in the open method.

4. What is the XMLHttpRequest method that actually sends the request to the URL specified?

a. retrieve
b. send
c. open
d. get

Explanation: The open method sets up the request by setting the URL, the GET or POST method, and whether or not you want to use asynchronous calls. It's the send method that actually performs the action.

Chapter 6: Working with JSON and MySQL

Objective: Because JSON is a data driven language, it's important to understand how it relates to databases. This chapter discovers how you use JSON with a MySQL database.

We mentioned before that JSON was a data driven format. It's meant for parsing information easily between applications. In most cases, the data created in a JSON file or request is created from information in a database. We'll focus on using JSON with the MySQL database, which is one of the most widely used databases on the Internet. It's an open-source platform, and most hosts give MySQL accounts to hosting users with certain contracts.

What is MySQL and How It Ties with JSON

MySQL is an open-source database that you can download directly and for free from the official MySQL website. If you've never worked with databases before, learning MySQL is a task in and of itself. It's difficult to get started with MySQL with little background, but we'll give you a small crash course, so you can understand how it relates to JSON objects.

First, you should understand the way MySQL stores data. MySQL uses tables to store information.

You can think of these tables as a spreadsheet. While a database is much more complex than a plain spreadsheet, viewing a table like a spreadsheet such as Excel makes it easier to understand when you're beginning your programming journey.

If you visualize an Excel spreadsheet, you can see a flat layout with columns and rows. The column headers group your fields, and each row is a record. The following is a simple representation of the way a spreadsheet looks.

FirstName	LastName	CustomerId
John	Smith	100
Joan	Smith	101

In the table above, we have three columns labeled FirstName, LastName, and CustomerId. There are two records, which are the rows that contain customer information. This layout is similar to a database table although much more complex code and calculations are used to store and retrieve data in a database than a spreadsheet.

Now, you might wonder how this table relates to JSON. Remember that JSON is an object of records. It represents a flat way to store code using brackets and variable-value pairs. Using the same example as the above, you should be able to visualize two records for a JSON object. The variable names would be FirstName, LastName, and CustomerId. The values would be the values you see in each record.

Let's take a look at how this table would look in JSON.

```
{
        { "FirstName" : "John", "LastName" : "Smith",
"CustomerId" : 100 },
```

{ "FirstName" : "Joan", "LastName" : "Smith",
"CustomerId" : 101 }
}

Notice that our JSON object contains a record for each row in the MySQL table representation. Each record is encapsulated by opening and closing brackets.

When you retrieve data, you first need a place to retrieve that data, and MySQL is one of the most common storage facilities. However, MySQL returns data in its own format and structure. For this reason, you have to build your own JSON object after you've retrieved the data. This is usually achieved using the programming language you choose for your backend processes. Since PHP is one of the most common backend programming languages, we'll show you how to query a MySQL database from a PHP page and then build a JSON object in PHP. Although the language you choose might be different, the concepts remain the same for building a JSON object.

Retrieving Data from MySQL

You first need a PHP editor to work with this code. Just like our HTML examples, we suggest using Notepad+ to use these examples.

The first step is to create your MySQL connection. You'll need a user name and password to connect to the MySQL database. The following code shows you how to connect to your MySQL database.

```
<?php
    $connection =
mysqli_connect("localhost","username","password","mydataba
se") or die("Error " . mysqli_error($connection));
```

```
$sql = "select * from customer";
   $result = mysqli_query($connection, $sql) or die("Query
Error " . mysqli_error($connection));
?>
```

Let's first take some time to understand what is happening in
this PHP code. The first line of code is the connection to the
database. You'll need to change username and password with
your own MySQL credentials. The "mydatabase" parameter is
the name of your database. "Localhost" is the standard for
host location, but check with your host to find out what host
name you need to enter for this parameter.

Next, the $sql variable contains the SQL query you want to
use. This query is responsible for retrieving records from the
database. Understanding MySQL code is beyond this ebook,
but you'll need to know SQL to query databases efficiently. In
this example, we get all customer records from the "customer"
table.

Finally, we run the query on the server and store the results in
the $result variable. The $result data is what we want to create
our JSON object, but MySQL and PHP return their own
format that we must change to our own JSON format.

Create an Array

Before we can switch data formats to an official JSON object,
we first need to change the MySQL results to a PHP array.

Remember that MySQL keeps records and columns in the
same format as a spreadsheet. The $result variable also has
this format. Before we can change it to JSON, we need to loop
through each record and build an array. Let's take a look at
how this happens in PHP.

```php
<?php
   $connection =
mysqli_connect("localhost","username","password","mydataba
se") or die("Error " . mysqli_error($connection));
   $sql = "select * from customer";
   $result = mysqli_query($connection, $sql) or die("Query
Error " . mysqli_error($connection));

   $myarray = array();
   while($row =mysqli_fetch_assoc($result))
   {
      $myarray[] = $row;
   }
?>
```

We added a while loop and the initialization of the array in
our code. The array first must be initialized, and that's what
we've done. We create an array named $myarray.

Once the array is created, we can now fill it with the MySQL
database information. The while loop tells PHP to loop
through each record as long as records are found during each
loop. In other words, once the while loop reaches the end of
the record set, it will terminate.

Each row in the record set is assigned a new position in the
array. If you recall from our array discussion, all arrays start
with an index position of 0 and then increment as a new
record is added. For instance, if the MySQL query returns 5
records, these five records are stored in the array at index
positions 0 to 4.

You don't need to worry about the index positions when you
use a loop to create your array.

The PHP language automatically increments the index during each iteration, so you just need to ensure that you loop through all records. Additionally, the PHP function mysqli_fetch_assoc handles the fetching for your records and incrementing to the next record. In other words, this function starts the process at the first MySQL record during the first loop. At the next loop, the function moves on to the next record and retrieves it. This function also detects when the end of the data set is reached, so the while loop can properly terminate. If you attempt to retrieve a record at a position that doesn't contain one, you will have errors in your PHP code.

We should also note that if no data is found in the $result variable, the while loop is skipped altogether. You'll need to code error checking for a data set with no records to alert the user that no records were found.

Using the Json_Encode Function

Now that you a functional array, you can use the json_encode function. This function is a handy addition to PHP that lets you automatically create a JSON object without much effort from you. This function translates an array to a valid JSON object.

Let's add the last component to our PHP script.

```
<?php
    $connection =
mysqli_connect("localhost","username","password","mydataba
se") or die("Error " . mysqli_error($connection));
    $sql = "select * from customer";
    $result = mysqli_query($connection, $sql) or die("Query
Error " . mysqli_error($connection));

    $myarray = array();
```

```php
    while($row =mysqli_fetch_assoc($result))
    {
        $myarray[] = $row;
    }

    $myjson = json_encode($myarray);
?>
```

That's all it takes! As you can see, the most difficult part of turning MySQL data sets into a JSON object is the actual retrieval from the database itself. It only takes one line of code to construct the JSON object, but it takes several to set up the database connect, query the database, and set up the array. PHP is one of the numerous languages that makes it easy to work with JSON data, which is why JSON is preferred by many programmers to transfer data.

We are still missing one piece to this code. We still need to close the database connection. This piece is often missed by new coders. If you leave too many open connections on a web server, you will eat away at resources. Additionally, the database server only allows a specific number of connections. Once the maximum is reached, the MySQL database begins to reject connections.

Let's add the line of code that closes the MySQL connection.

```php
<?php
    $connection =
mysqli_connect("localhost","username","password","mydataba
se") or die("Error " . mysqli_error($connection));
    $sql = "select * from customer";
    $result = mysqli_query($connection, $sql) or die("Query
Error " . mysqli_error($connection));

    $myarray = array();
```

```php
while($row =mysqli_fetch_assoc($result))
{
    $myarray[] = $row;
}

$myjson = json_encode($myarray);

mysqli_close($connection);

?>
```

That's all it takes to query a MySQL database, create a JSON object, and then correctly close the database connection.

There's one last thing that we should add to our code. We probably want to verify that the JSON object was properly created. We can use an echo statement to view the JSON object in the browser. Let's add this echo statement to our code.

```php
<?php
    $connection =
mysqli_connect("localhost","username","password","mydataba
se") or die("Error " . mysqli_error($connection));
    $sql = "select * from customer";
    $result = mysqli_query($connection, $sql) or die("Query
Error " . mysqli_error($connection));

    $myarray = array();
    while($row =mysqli_fetch_assoc($result))
    {
        $myarray[] = $row;
    }

$myjson = json_encode($myarray);
echo $myjson;
mysqli_close($connection);
```

?>

Now we can see what happens after the JSON object is created. Assuming we have the same data set as the MySQL table we illustrated previously, you should see the following output in the browser.

```
{
       { "FirstName" : "John", "LastName" : "Smith",
"CustomerId" : 100 },
       { "FirstName" : "Joan", "LastName" : "Smith",
"CustomerId" : 101 }
}
```

It might not be as formatted as we have above, but the syntax should be the same. If you get nothing printed to the browser, it's possible that you have no data returned from the MySQL database. It's also possible that the JSON was not properly created.

If you think that the JSON transformation caused an error, you might need to do some troubleshooting. Ensure that the MySQL query returns data. You can do this by querying the MySQL database manually. If no records return, this is your issue and you'll need to change your query.

If records are returned, revisit the while loop and identify if any errors are caused during the loop. You can use echo statements to help identify any issues with your iterations.

Building a JSON File Instead

We've mentioned several times that you can store JSON content in an external file. This file typically has the json file extension, but you can use any text-based extension.

As long as you can access the file from the web server, you can use the JSON file to manipulate your data.

You can use the same code as above except let's change the output to a file instead. This file will contain the same output as our echo statement.

Let's first remove the statements that we don't need and copy and paste the code that would do need to create a JSON file.

```php
<?php
    $connection =
mysqli_connect("localhost","username","password","mydatabase") or die("Error " . mysqli_error($connection));
    $sql = "select * from customer";
    $result = mysqli_query($connection, $sql) or die("Query Error " . mysqli_error($connection));

    $myarray = array();
    while($row =mysqli_fetch_assoc($result))
    {
        $myarray[] = $row;
    }

    $myjson = json_encode($myarray);
    mysqli_close($connection);

?>
```

You'll notice that we only removed one line of code – the echo code. Instead of printing results to the browser, let's look at the code to create a file.

```php
<?php
```

```php
    $connection =
mysqli_connect("localhost","username","password","mydataba
se") or die("Error " . mysqli_error($connection));
    $sql = "select * from customer";
    $result = mysqli_query($connection, $sql) or die("Query
Error " . mysqli_error($connection));

    $myarray = array();
    while($row =mysqli_fetch_assoc($result))
    {
        $myarray[] = $row;
    }

    $myjson = json_encode($myarray);

$fp = fopen('customers.json', 'w');
    fwrite($fp, $myjson);
    fclose($fp);

    mysqli_close($connection);

?>
```

Notice that we added three lines of code after the json_encode function. The first line of code opens a file. The file name is customers.json. The "w" parameter tells PHP that you want to open the file to write to it. If you used "r" as the parameter, you would only be able to read the file.

Next is the fwrite function. This function writes the information to a file, which in this case is customers.json. Notice that the data we used is stored in the $myjson variable, which is the variable that contains the JSON object we build from the array using json_encode.

Finally, we close the file. This is just as important as closing the database connection. If you don't close the file after opening it, the operating system keeps a lock on it. This lock must be released before you can open or write more information to the file. This is why it's important to always close files from your code.

Working with MySQL and JSON is an important part of understanding how to program web applications. If you work with JSON, you'll always need to work with some kind of database used to store and retrieve data.

Lab Questions

1. When learning MySQL, what is the best way to describe the architecture of a database table?

a. Spreadsheet
b. Word document
c. PowerPoint presentation
d. HTML file

Explanation: A spreadsheet is a good way to visualize the layout of a MySQL database when you learn storage and retrieval of data.

2. When building a JSON object in PHP, what must you do first before you can encode the data to JSON format?

a. Close the database connection
b. Open a file
c. Print the data
d. Turn the data to an array

Before you can use the internal PHP function to transform data to a JSON object, it first must be converted to an array.

3. What is the function that lets you turn a PHP array to a JSON object?

a. encode()
b. json_encode()
c. json()
d. jencode()

Explanation: The json_encode function takes a PHP array and automatically transforms it into a valid JSON object.

4. After you query the MySQL database from your PHP page, what must you do before you end the code?

a. Close the database connection
b. Open a file
c. Print the data
d. Turn the data to an array

Explanation: If you don't close the database connection, you will eventually run out of accepted connections and the database will refuse the queries.

Chapter 7: Using JSON with jQuery and Ajax

Objective: This chapter discusses how you can work with jQuery and Ajax to parse and retrieve JSON data from within your web pages.

In the last chapter, we discussed the way you can grab data from your MySQL database and build a JSON object. This is the first step towards making complete web applications use JSON as the data transformation component. Once you create the PHP page (or whatever language you prefer to use), it's time to build the frontend HTML page that calls the PHP processing page. Typically, you use jQuery and Ajax to make asynchronous calls to the server. The PHP page illustrates the backend design for the web call, but you now need a way for your frontend HTML pages to retrieve and display the data. We'll show you how to work with JSON, Ajax and jQuery in this chapter.

What is Ajax and jQuery?

We mentioned that JSON is usually implemented with JavaScript code. Ajax and jQuery are both JavaScript libraries. They are similar but not the same.

They both let you create asynchronous calls. This is especially important when you're creating fast and efficient web applications. The user experience is much faster when you use JavaScript to process data.

It's even faster when you can create asynchronous calls instead of forcing a complete reload of all elements on the page. We discussed the way asynchronous calls are made in chapter 5.

To briefly review the previous asynchronous discussion, remember that a typical synchronous call-back to a web server forces the browser to refresh the entire page of information. That means any footer, header, navigation and sidebars are reloaded, refreshed, and even dynamically queried on the server. This takes resources from the web server, and users have to wait for your pages to reload after they submit data.

With asynchronous communication, you send the user input to the web application's processing page without forcing a reload of the pages in your user's browser. The process takes fewer resources from the server, and your users have a better experience with your web application.

Ajax and jQuery both let you create asynchronous calls to a web server. They are both JavaScript libraries, but they are not the same libraries. jQuery is a framework that actually uses Ajax. jQuery makes querying the HTML document easier, and you can manipulate information on the web page from the client side.

Ajax is an asynchronous JavaScript library. We've actually used Ajax in Chapter 5 when we used the XMLHttpRequest object.

Both of these frameworks are extremely useful especially when you want to work with JSON information. You'll use jQuery and Ajax a lot as a web developer. It's a required language for most developers, and it works within HTML so you don't need to know a specific backend language to know jQuery and Ajax.

Both of these frameworks are used in conjunction with any backend language including PHP, C#, Java and VB.

One final note on jQuery and Ajax: they are separate libraries that must be downloaded and included in your HTML pages. We haven't included them up until now. You can download the libraries from the official jQuery and Ajax websites, or you can use a cloud host and link to the libraries. For instance, Google lets you use their servers as a host for jQuery libraries. Just link the library into your HTML pages and you're ready to work with the frameworks.

Retrieving JSON Data in Ajax and jQuery

Now that you have a background for Ajax and jQuery, it's time to see the code needed to query a database from a frontend web application. Since we know that JSON works with frontend applications, we know that we need to return to the HTML page template. Copy and paste the template below.

```
<!DOCTYPE html>
<html>
<head>
<script src="jquery-1.11.3.min.js"></script>
</head>
<body>

<h2>JSON User Account Example</h2>

<p id="myuser"></p>

<script>

</script>

</body>
</html>
```

You might notice that we added another line of code to the HTML template. The script tag is a link to our JavaScript jQuery libraries. You'll need this link to effectively use jQuery. In this example, we've downloaded the jQuery file and hosted it locally on our web server. You can also use an external URL to pull in the necessary jQuery libraries. If your web server is slow and suffering from performance issues, it's better to use a cloud host such as Google or Amazon to host and link to jQuery libraries.

We first need to override the event that will trigger the jQuery and Ajax submissions. In this example, we have no form or input button, so we'll use the "document ready" event. This event occurs when the HTML page loads in the web browser. After the page is finished loading, this event is triggered. We can override this event and automatically begin our JSON processing procedure.

Let's add the code to the script tag.

```
<!DOCTYPE html>
<html>
<head>
<script src="jquery-1.11.3.min.js"></script>
</head>
<body>

<h2>JSON User Account Example</h2>

<p id="myuser"></p>

<script>
$(document).ready(function () {
```

```
});
</script>

</body>
</html>
```

The above function is jQuery syntax. Notice that we create our own function and override the ready event. After the page fully loads, any JavaScript code within the brackets and parenthesis will execute. Now let's add the Ajax function to query the web server.

```
<!DOCTYPE html>
<html>
<head>
<script src="jquery-1.11.3.min.js"></script>
</head>
<body>

<h2>JSON User Account Example</h2>

<p id="myuser"></p>

<script>
$(document).ready(function () {
$.ajax({
        type: 'GET',
        url:
'http://mydomain.com/json_process.php',
        data: { user_account_id: '100' },
        success: function (data) {
            var user = data
            $('#myuser').html(data);
        }
    });
```

```
});
</script>

</body>
</html>
```

We just added a ton of new code to the document ready function. Let's take the processing step by step so we can understand the way this Ajax function works.

First we have the Ajax specification call. This tells the JavaScript library that you want to use Ajax for the function. Since this is an Ajax specific function, we need to specify to the web browser that we need Ajax. Remember that you need to download and include the Ajax libraries in your HTML pages, which we've included in the above template.

The first line of code within the Ajax call is the "type" attribute. If you remember from previous chapters, we specified the GET form submission when we want to send data in the query string variables. The other form submission type is POST. The POST type is preferred, but some developers use GET while they code their programs. Using the GET procedure lets you view the data while you post it back and forth from the web server. In other words, it's a good testing and debugging tool as you code your applications. In this example, we've used the GET type, but just know that most of your applications should use POST. If you work in the development field, you will see most developers use POST in their jQuery functions.

The next line of code in the Ajax function is the URL. You need this in any Ajax call to an external web server. You can call a web page on your local server or on an external web server. In this example, we are querying a domain named mydomain.com.

We then point to a PHP processing page on the web server named json_process.php.

After you specify the URL, you need to specify the data that you want to pass to the processing page. In the URL attribute, we only set up the processing page. We didn't specify the data that we want to send, and this is what the "data" attribute is for. We only send one piece of information in the data attribute, but you can send multiple pieces of information. Remember the JSON object variable format? This attribute takes the same format. You send variable-value pairs separated by commas. The data even has the opening and closing brackets, because the format we're using is JSON. In this example, we're sending a user account. The intention is to get the user account information from the MySQL database using the processing page as an intermediate.

The success attribute sets the function that should be called when the processing page is successful. We don't have it specified in this code, but you can also call a specific function if the processing page fails. This is Ajax's way of performing error handling on the data passed to the page. Error handling is an entire topic on its own, and it can get confusing. To avoid confusion, we're skipping the error handling code to keep it simple to learn.

You'll notice the "data" variable passed in the success function. This is the data returned by the processing page. This data can be in any type of format. It doesn't necessarily need to be JSON. In fact, you can retrieve and entire HTML page and print the data on the current HTML page, but this because tedious and difficult. For this reason, developers prefer retrieving JSON information.

In this example, we've simple sent the output to the myuser div tag.

This means that you'll see the JSON object as a whole on the page, which is probably not what you want to do. You want to format the output to make it user friendly.

Let's change the code to be more user friendly and formatted using what we know of how we can use JSON syntax.

```html
<!DOCTYPE html>
<html>
<head>
<script src="jquery-1.11.3.min.js"></script>
</head>
<body>

<h2>JSON User Account Example</h2>

<p id="myuser"></p>

<script>
$(document).ready(function () {
$.ajax({
        type: 'GET',
        url:
'http://mydomain.com/json_process.php',
        data: { user_account_id: '100' },
        success: function (data) {
            var user = data
            var firstname = user.FirstName;
            var lastname = user.LastName;
            var accounted = user.AccountId;
            var output = "First Name: " + firstname
+ "<br>" +
                "Last Name: " + lastname + "<br>"
+
                "Account Id: " + accounted;
            $('#myuser').html(output);
        }
    });
```

```
});
</script>

</body>
</html>
```

This produces a much more user friendly output. We've built a string based on the information we retrieved from the processing page, Remember that this assumes the data format retrieved is JSON, but since we coded the json_process page in the last chapter, we know that we've used JSON as our main data format.

Notice that we were able to use the JSON object values and variable names to retrieve data. We use this data to build a string one by one filled with the JSON information. After the string is built, we can then show the output to the user. To make the data format well, we also use the "<br>" HTML tags. These tags are used to create a carriage return on the page. The "<br>" tag stands for "break," which makes it easy to remember when you want to know how to add a line break in your code.

Using the $.getJSON Function Instead

The above method is the standard way to retrieve data, but you have one other option. You can use the $.getJSON function to get JSON data from a processing page. Again, you need to ensure that the data returned is indeed JSON, so this function only works with JSON input and output. Let's change our current HTML page to use the $.getJSON function.

```
<!DOCTYPE html>
<html>
<head>
<script src="jquery-1.11.3.min.js"></script>
```

```
</head>
<body>

<h2>JSON User Account Example</h2>

<p id="myuser"></p>

<script>
$(document).ready(function () {
$.getJSON('http://mydomain.com/json_process.php',
{ user_account_id: '100' }, function(data) {
    var user = data
            var firstname = user.FirstName;
            var lastname = user.LastName;
            var accounted = user.AccountId;
            var output = "First Name: " + firstname
+ "<br>" +
                "Last Name: " + lastname + "<br>"
+
                "Account Id: " + accounted;
            $('#myuser').html(output);
});
});
</script>

</body>
</html>
```

We've eliminated some code using the $.getJSON method. This method is becoming more popular in development circles. It makes it much easier to query data from an external process and use it to display data. Both methods are valid, so you can pick and choose which one works right for you.

JSON, jQuery and Ajax go hand in hand when it comes to front end web development. You'll certainly run into this type of query when you start any type of development position.

Since Ajax and jQuery have functionality that works directly with JSON, it's often the triad of choice for development projects.

What's great about this code is that it's a real-world example of what you'll see when you take on your first coding project. Just remember that you'll be responsible for writing the frontend JavaScript code as well as the processing page, so you're forced to use JSON in multiple languages when you work in web application development.

Lab Question

1. What do you need to do before you can use jQuery in your web pages?

a. Add the Ajax library
b. Add the jQuery library
c. Query the MySQL server
d. Create a processing page

Explanation: The jQuery libraries are a framework of the JavaScript engine, but you must link the library files to your HTML pages before you can use them.

2. What type of web calls are made using Ajax libraries?

a. asynchronous
b. synchronous
c. flat
d. transport

Explanation: Ajax libraries let you make asynchronous calls to a web server, which reduces load times and makes your web pages more user friendly.

3. What function do you use to after you retrieve data from the processing page?

a. success
b. fail
c. finished
d. complete

Explanation: The success function property in an Ajax call lets you customize the way that your JSON information is displayed in the web page.

4. What function do you use if the PHP processing page isn't successful or gives you an error when you attempt to query data?

a. success
b. fail
c. finished
d. complete

Explanation: the fail function property is used when your pages aren't successful and you must perform error handling in your Ajax calls.

5. What is the most common submission type when using Ajax functions to send data to a processing page?

a. get
b. post
c. send
d. retrieve

Explanation: Although we used the GET method in our example code, the most common method used in most jQuery and Ajax coding methods is the POST method. The GET method sends data using the URL's query string, which is considered more insecure and less efficient than the POST method.

6. If you want to run an Ajax query as soon as the page loads, what event do you need to override?

a. document.load
b. document.html
c. document.ready
d. document.unload

Explanation: The document.ready event happens when you load a web page and finishes its loading process. You override this event to immediately run a function after the page loads.

7. We built an Ajax query to submit data to a processing page. Write the code that sends data to a PHP processing page using Ajax.

```
$.ajax({
    type: 'GET',
    url:
'http://mydomain.com/json_process.php',
    data: { user_account_id: '100' },
    success: function (data) {
        var user = data
        $('#myuser').html(data);
    }
});
```

<u>Explanation:</u> The above code sends a user account number to a processing page named json_process.php and data is printed to the myuser paragraph tag.

Chapter 8: JSON and PHP

Objective: Some programming languages work natively with the JSON language. This chapter covers the way PHP and JSON work together to transfer data.

We've covered several different ways to use JSON, but now you need to know how to use JSON with specific languages. The first language you'll likely run into as a web developer is the PHP language. This language is one of the most widely used languages. It's open-source, and it's free to use. Because of these two benefits, it's a favorite among programmers learning a language for web development.

PHP is similar to the C language, so if you understand a C language, you can probably jump into PHP coding. It's a good starting point as a developer if you want to create web applications. While JSON is a much more simple language than other languages, PHP is much more complex and needs time to learn. PHP has several frameworks and libraries that you can use to make coding a PHP platform much easier especially for a beginner.

Since PHP is completely free, you can set up your working environment with no costs to you. Even MySQL is free, so it costs nothing to set up the database environment you need for dynamic coding and storage. Take this into account when you determine how you want to build your programs. You can choose the open-source route, or you can used closed-source or compiled languages such as C#. Once you choose the language, you must stick to it, so choose wisely.

Most programmers stick with their favorite language and continue to build on an existing project with the same language. It's very difficult to build a platform on multiple languages especially when you're first starting out and learning any language including the JSON format syntax.

Set Up the Page

When you work with PHP, you have to decide what environment you want to use. We suggested in previous chapters that you should download the Notepad+ application. This application is beneficial for developers on a budget, because it's free, and it recognizes several other languages besides PHP. The great thing about Notepad+ is that is color codes your PHP statements, so you can more easily recognize strings, functions, and any other data types. Most coders prefer color coded programming environments to make it easier and more efficient to code.

For the PHP part of the page, you don't need any specific opening and closing tags like HTML. You just need the PHP indicators, which encapsulate your code. The following is the basic PHP "template" when you begin coding.

```
<?php

?>
```

It seems simple, but it's an important part of setting up a PHP page to begin programming.

Before you start working with PHP, it's important to know some important basics. While we can't give you a full tutorial of PHP in one chapter, we can give you some basics when you want to work with the JSON object format.

First, PHP is an interpreted language, so you don't need to compile any of your code. However, you do need the interpreter on your development machine and on your web server. Most web hosts offer PHP services on their servers. As long as it's a paid service, you should have PHP capabilities on the host machine. Even Windows servers have the PHP interpreter installed, so you can use PHP on an IIS system. It's not recommended, but the servers are capable.

To work with a database, you need that database installed as well. If you recall from chapter 6, we worked with the MySQL database. If you decide to work with a database and these projects, you need to install the database server on your local development machine and the web server. Check with your web host about MySQL databases. Most hosting services include at least one MySQL database. You can use this database to store your JSON data.

Finally, you should test your development environment before you get started with PHP. You can write a simple echo statement ensure that PHP is running smoothly on your development machine, and you can ensure that you can view any output you place in your pages. Let's take a look at a short verification script.

```
<?php
        echo "Hello World";
?>
```

This statement prints "Hello World" on the user's browser. If PHP is not working correctly, you won't see anything or PHP will show you an error. If this happens, you should review your PHP installation and review the documentation.

Encoding and Decoding JSON in PHP

PHP is extremely useful when working with PHP because the language has its own internal encoding and decoding functions. Encoding JSON means to take an array and turn it into JSON. We covered creating an array in PHP in previous chapters. Decoding JSON means to take a current JSON object and turning it into a usable string. We briefly covered decoding functions in previous chapters as well.

We'll start with encoding JSON in a PHP object. We discussed and reviewed JSON objects, but what about PHP objects?

PHP objects are much different than JSON objects. PHP lets you create classes. Classes are also referred to as objects. Classes represent a part of your program. For instance, suppose you were creating a customer service portal. You need to create each section of the customer service portal. These sections would represent classes. The objects you would create would be customers, orders, products and any other component that makes up your customer portal. This, of course, takes some preparation, design and engineering before you put it into practice, but you can eventually figure out how to design your classes or objects once you properly design your component structures.

Before we can encode an object into JSON, we need to create the object. Let's create a customer object in PHP to help work with the encoding function. Let's take a look at some code first.

```php
<?php
class Customer {
    public $firstname = "";
    public $accountId  = "";
    public $lastname = "";
 }
?>
```

That's all it takes to create a class in PHP. The class or object name is Customer. You then have the opening bracket that tells the PHP language that the class properties are beginning.

The next three lines of code are the properties for the class. We set the properties with a blank string value. You don't have to set the values to blank strings if you don't want to. You can also set them to a default value. This default value is used when you don't define a value when you call the class or initialize it.

The above code just creates the class. It doesn't do anything with the class. You need to initialize the class and work with its methods and properties before you can encode it into JSON. Note that this class object doesn't have any methods, so there isn't much to do with any actions. Normally, a class has methods that perform actions. For instance, a Customer class might have a method that inserts a new customer into the database, edit the customer information, or even deactivate a customer account in the database.

With the class created, we now need to initialize the class. Let's initialize the Customer class and define some information that we'll assign to the class properties.

```php
<?php
class Customer {
    public $firstname = "";
    public $accountId  = "";
    public $lastname = "";
}

$e = new Customer ();
    $e->firstname = "john";
    $e->lastname  = "smith";
    $e->accounted = 199;
```

```
?>
```

Notice that we put our code outside of the class open and close brackets. This is because we don't want to add it to the class itself. The class only represents the information that concerns a customer, and we need to initialize the object outside of the class structure.

The first line of code initializes the object. This line of code is not unlike when we created the XMLHttpRequest object in previous chapters. The object is initialized and assigned to a variable named $e. You can give your variables any name. We are just using $e to make it easy to identify.

The next three lines of code are used to assign values to the class properties. We've assigned a first name, last name, and an account Id to our customer object. Note that objects are reusable, so you can continue to initialize the class and create a new object with different values. You aren't limited to one object within the code. Each object is its own container, so you can create one or hundred objects in your code. Just know that each time you create an object, the system must allocate memory for the object and its data. This can be costly overhead for your web server, so only initialize objects when you need them.

Now that you have your object built, you can encode it. Remember when we encoded the array from the MySQL database? We can use the same encoding function to encode our object. Let's take a look at that code.

```php
<?php
class Customer {
    public $firstname = "";
    public $accountId  = "";
    public $lastname = "";
```

```php
}

$e = new Customer ();
  $e->firstname = "john";
  $e->lastname  = "smith";
  $e->accounted = 199;

$myvar = json_encode($e);

?>
```

As you can see, we only added one line of code to our PHP page. But this one line of code does an important part of the JSON encoding methods. The object is encoded and then assigned to the $myvar variable. We still need to see the output, so let's take a look at the results with the echo statement. If you recall, we used the echo statement in our previous chapter to review the results of a JSON encoding.

```php
<?php
class Customer {
    public $firstname = "";
    public $accountId  = "";
    public $lastname = "";
  }

$e = new Customer ();
  $e->firstname = "john";
  $e->lastname  = "smith";
  $e->accounted = 199;

$myvar = json_encode($e);
echo $myvar;
?>
```

When the system prints out the JSON object, you should see the following JSON object printout.

{ "firstname" : "john", "lastname" : "smith", "accounted" : 199 }

Now that you've encoded your string, you can decode it as well. PHP has a decoding function as well. You just need a string of JSON variables. We can use the string that we have above to decode the values.

Let's take a look at what a decoding function looks like in PHP when you want to use JSON.

```php
<?php
class Customer {
    public $firstname = "";
    public $accountId  = "";
    public $lastname = "";
  }

$e = new Customer ();
  $e->firstname = "john";
  $e->lastname  = "smith";
  $e->accounted = 199;

$myvar = json_encode($e);
 echo "Encoded: " .$myvar;

echo "Decoded: ".var_dump(json_decode($myvar));

?>
```

We just added the json_decode function to our code. This function decodes the encoded JSON object we created. The output is completely different than what we would use in an encoding function. Let's take a look at what we should see when we use this function.

```
array(5) {
   ["firstname"] => john
   ["lastname"] => smith
   ["accounted"] => 199
}
```

Notice that the output is much different than our JSON output. That's because the JSON output is a JSON object and formatted in the JSON object syntax. When you decode a JSON object, it doesn't automatically transform back into the Customer object. Instead, the output is changed to an array. This is why we used the var_dump function to print out the output from the JSON object. The var_dump variable is used to print out a list of array values. Since the json_decode function transforms the JSON object into an array, we need this function to parse the results and print them to the browser.

We can't forget our HTML file that calls the PHP file. Let's take a look at what this would look like.

```
<!DOCTYPE html>
<html>
<head>
<script src="jquery-1.11.3.min.js"></script>
```

```
</head>
<body>

<h2>JSON User Account Example</h2>

<p id="myuser"></p>

<script>
$(document).ready(function () {
$.getJSON('http://mydomain.com/json_process.php',
{ }, function(data) {
    var user = data
            var firstname = user.FirstName;
            var lastname = user.LastName;
            var accounted = user.AccountId;
            var output = "First Name: " + firstname
+ "<br>" +
                "Last Name: " + lastname + "<br>"
+
                "Account Id: " + accounted;
            $('#myuser').html(output);
});
});
</script>

</body>
</html>
```

Notice that we're using the same HTML page as the previous chapter. Remember that JSON is universal, so you can use any language as the processing page. This assumes that you name the processing page json_process.php and upload it to your domain's web server.

We don't need to send any information to the processing page, because we aren't querying a MySQL database and need any user input. We just want a customer that we assigned in the processing page. Remember to remove the decoded values, but this HTML page will take any JSON output. You can, however, use any HTML output if you decide to switch to HTML output from the processing page.

Now that you can see how to work with JSON and PHP, you can build dynamic web pages that allow you to asynchronously make calls to processing pages. If you're wondering when you can use something like this, consider a login form. Instead of making the user wait for the login page to process, you can display an Ajax login screen and send the input to the web server without reloading the entire page. You can still redirect the user if you wanted to display a successful account screen, or you can display a login failed error message when the user enters the wrong username and password.

If you decide to get into development, you'll need to know how to work with JSON, PHP and HTML static pages. All of these are necessary when creating robust, dynamic, and well performing applications.

Lab Questions

1. What is the correct PHP syntax to create a PHP class named Customer?

```php
class Customer {
  public $firstname = "";
  public $accountId = "";
  public $lastname = "";
}
```

Explanation: The class operator defines a class. Any properties within the class object are considered properties in the object oriented programming world.

2. Write the code that encodes a Customer object named $e and assigns the object to a variable.

$myvar = json_encode($e);

Explanation: The json_encode function encodes a class and assigns the value to a variable. In this example, we assign the encoded value to the variable named $myvar.

3. When you want to decode a JSON object, what does PHP automatically decode the object to?

a. an array
b. a class
c. a JSON object
d. a string

Explanation: The PHP decode process automatically transforms a JSON object into an array that you can print out using the var_dump function.

4. What is the PHP function used to decode a JSON object?

a. json_encode
b. json_decode
c. decode
d. json

Explanation: The json_decode function takes a JSON object and transforms it into an array variable.

5. Write the code that prints Hello World to the browser so you can test your PHP installation.

echo "Hello World";

<u>Explanation:</u> The echo statement prints output to the browser.

Chapter 9: JSON in Python

Objective: Python is becoming a popular language in the web and scripting world. This chapter shows you how to use JSON with the Python language.

It was rumored that Google uses Python for its search engine crawler. The result was that several people decided to make Python their language of choice. The result is that a lot of people use Python as a main form of their scripting language. Python is a modular language, which means that you need to install libraries from its repository before you can use certain functions. One such function is the JSON library. You'll need to install an extra library to get these coding examples to work.

You might wonder why you would use JSON in a scripting language that doesn't display output to users. But JSON is data driven and doesn't care about the language you use it with. For instance, you might want to use Python to automate some database functionality. Python works with any database language, but it's mostly used with MySQL or Oracle. You can also use it with Microsoft SQL Server. Remember that the database and language don't matter to JSON. It can be used in any platform completely independent of the language used.

Set Up Python

Python doesn't have any natural libraries in earlier versions to parse JSON like PHP and C#.

You need to download the library into your Python environment if you have a version older than 2.6. If you have 2.6 or earlier, you can use the internal Python JSON library.

The library you use for JSON and Python in earlier versions is called simplejson. Simplejson works very similarly to the natural Python libraries you get with earlier versions. You can find instructions on how to use simplejson on their website, but we'll cover how to use older versions of Python interpreters with simplejson examples. The commands used in both older versions of Python and the newer libraries work the same.

We'll combine both the older and newer examples within this chapter. For each example, you need to import the JSON library you need to automatically parse any of the JSON strings and objects we use.

You add your imports at the top of any JSON code. If you are using the earlier versions of JSON, add this to the top of all pages where you import and parse JSON.

Import json

If you are using older versions of JSON, you need to import the simplejson libraries. The following statement should be added to all Python scripts.

Import simplejson as json

Notice that the second line of code is using an alias. An alias is a way to add shorthand to your statements. With the first statement, the JSON library is imported without any alias. In the second example, the simplejson has an alias of json. This means that we can use the keyword json to call our imported library.

This is what makes both the simplejson and the regular json library work with the code that we're about to use.

Simple Python and JSON

First, we need a string to work with. This is assuming that you've been passed a string value that's properly set up in the JSON syntax. For most Python projects, you'll import data from some external API, user, or another script.

Let's take a look at a JSON string in Python.

json_string = '{"firstname" : "John", "lastname" : "Smith" }'

You'll notice that we're using the same string we've used in previous chapters, except in this example we've enclosed the JSON object in tick marks. We usually enclose our strings in quotes, but we have quotes in the JSON object. With Python, you can also use the tick mark to enclose strings. You use these tick marks to enclose strings when you're using quote characters with your JSON object variable names.

Now that we have our string, we need to know the Python function that parses the JSON object. Python uses the library we imported earlier, and the "loads" function from that library. Let's take a look at the code to convert the string to a JSON object.

import json
parsed_json = json.loads(json_string)

That's it! That's all it takes to parse JSON in Python. It's extremely easy and Python does all the work for you.

Notice that we first imported the JSON library. This library is what's needed to automated many of the functions. If you didn't use this library, you'd have to parse the string character by character using your own functions and loops.

Next is the json.loads function. This function automates the parsing functionality. As long as the JSON string is formatted properly, the function will work. If you give it an incorrectly formatted JSON string, the function returns an error. We then assign the results to the parse_json variable. This variable becomes a JSON object that we can then work with.

We have the parsed data, so now we want to display it. You use the JSON object's variable name just like you used in other chapters. Let's take a look at what this parsed data looks like and what you can do to print it in the display.

```
print(parsed_json['firstname'])
```

That's all it takes to print the JSON object value. In this example, we use the Python print function to display the data. Notice that Python uses a different notation than other languages for calling a JSON variable. Python uses the variable name with opening and closing brackets along with the variable name in tick marks. This tells Python to get the value from the "firstname" JSON object variable and display it to the user.

What happens when you want to view the entire JSON object? Python's JSON library also has the functionality to print all variables and values from a JSON object to the display. Let's take a look at the code.

```
print(json.dumps(parsed_json))
```

The json.dumps function is a way to take a JSON object and print all content to the screen. This is a quick way to display your information especially when you want to verify that the JSON object is valid and does not have any errors. It also checks to ensure that the JSON object has a value contained, so you're not working with a null object.

Working with Python, Classes and JSON

We showed you how to work with PHP classes and covert them to JSON objects in the last chapter. You can do the same with Python and its classes.

Before you can start converting classes to JSON objects, you must learn how to create a class in Python. Let's take a look at a class we'll call Customer just like the last chapter.

```
class Customer(object):
    def __init__(self, firstname, lastname):
        self.firstname = firstname
        self.lastname = lastname
```

This is a class structure in Python. If you've ever looked at other languages, this type of class initialization is different than other C level programming languages.

The first line of code indicates that you want to create a class. You know this from the "class" statement. Next is the name of the class. In this example, we want to create a class named Customer. Just like any other definition statement in Python, it's followed by a colon.

The next line of code initializes the class and defines the parameters needed to create the object.

The self-statement is an interpreter specific statement. It is meant to allow the class to "talk" to itself. You don't need to know too much about the self-keyword other than you use it to assign variables to the class during initialization and when you run methods from within the class.

Next is the class code structure. We have no methods in this class, because we don't want to make it too complicated. We just want to create a class with a couple of properties to get a good idea of how classes work with JSON objects. We define two properties. We define a firstname property and a lastname property. Both of these properties use the "self" designation to tell the interpreter that any values sent to the initialization function should be assigned to the class' own properties. All you need to know for this lesson is that the self-designation points to the current class, and it's a useful way to keep your class code clean without causing confusion between external variables and internal variables.

Notice that the values used in the initialization function are also assigned to the class properties. When you pass a first name and last name value to the class when you create it, these values are assigned to the class properties, so you can retrieve them later in your code.

With our class created, we can now create a class in our Python code. Let's take a look at how this works.

```
class Customer(object):
    def __init__(self, firstname, lastname):
        self.firstname = firstname
        self.lastname = lastname
user = Customer ('John', 'Smith')
```

We added a line of code after our class statement. This line of code initializes the class statement and assigns it to the user variable. You'll probably notice that there is no specific process in Python to create a variable explicitly. Most languages make you initialize the variable first, and then you can assign it a value. Python just lets you create a variable name with no initialization and then assign it a value. The Python interpreter just knows that what is being assigned is a class initialized and any of the values are placed in the user variable.

Now let's identify with the initialization code is doing. We're passing the Customer class initialization object the name "John Smith." This variable information is passed to the Customer class, and then the "self" notation tells the class initialization statements to assign the values John and Smith respectively to the corresponding variable names "firstname" and "lastname."

So now that we have our class defined, we need to turn the class into a JSON object. Let's take a look at the code that takes this class and turns it into an object.

```
import json
class Customer(object):
    def __init__(self, firstname, lastname):
        self.firstname = firstname
        self.lastname = lastname
user = Customer ('John', 'Smith')

json.dumps(user)
```

Notice that we added the import notation at the top of the code. Remember that you need to import the JSON library when you want to encode and decode any JSON objects. The result of the printout is the following.

'{"firstname" : "John", "lastname" : "Smith" }'

In some cases, the above code fails. You should take precautions when dumping Python classes without having any type of error correction. To correct the situation, let's change the above code to compensate for any issues we could have with the JSON transformation.

```
import json
class Customer(object):
    def __init__(self, firstname, lastname):
        self.firstname = firstname
        self.lastname = lastname
user = Customer ('John', 'Smith')

def jdefault(o):
    return o.__dict__

print(json.dumps(user, default=jdefault))
```

What the above code does is check for any errors. We've added a jdefault function to parse through any errors and identify if the conversion will cause any issues. You'll know if the JSON conversion failed, because the following error is returned from Python.

```
Traceback (most recent call last):
  File "<stdin>", line 1, in <module>
  File "/usr/lib/python3.3/json/__init__.py", line 236, in dumps
    return _default_encoder.encode(obj)
  File "/usr/lib/python3.3/json/encoder.py", line 191, in encode
    chunks = self.iterencode(o, _one_shot=True)
  File "/usr/lib/python3.3/json/encoder.py", line 249, in iterencode
```

```
    return _iterencode(o, 0)
  File "/usr/lib/python3.3/json/encoder.py", line 173, in
default
    raise TypeError(repr(o) + " is not JSON serializable")
TypeError: <__main__.Customer object at 0x7f2eccc88150> is
not JSON serializable
```

For someone who isn't used to programming, these types of errors can be confusing. The important part of the error is in the last line where it says "… is not JSON serializable." This error is telling you that the JSON library parser is unable to detect the proper syntax and format of the class and can't "serialize" the object. Serialization is a programming term that turns an object such as a class into a readable string. In this case, we want to turn the object into a readable JSON object string.

Let's go back to our code.

```
import json
class Customer(object):
    def __init__(self, firstname, lastname):
        self.firstname = firstname
        self.lastname = lastname
user = Customer ('John', 'Smith')

def jdefault(o):
    return o.__dict__

print(json.dumps(user, default=jdefault))
```

As you can see, converting JSON in Python is easier than even PHP. The default function traps any errors, and you can then view your class objects in JSON format.

Python is primarily used for scripting and automation, so you'll need to work with JSON if you use Python for transferring data. It's especially useful when you work with Python and a database environment. You can retrieve the data from any database such as MySQL, Oracle, or SQL Server, load the content in the same way you did with PHP and then create a JSON object. The JSON object is then sent to the calling application or stored in a file. Since JSON is mostly used for automation, you'll have large data sets that you need to work with, but Python is a lightweight

You'll notice from this chapter that it doesn't matter what language you use. JSON's format and syntax always stays the same. The only thing that changes is the way you decode and encode the JSON object. In the last chapter, a string was converted and in this chapter a string was converted. This back and forth concept is what makes JSON so useful for automation, web applications and even mobile applications.

Lab Questions

1. What version of Python has an internal library you can use to convert JSON objects?

a. 2.1
b. 2.2
c. 2.5
d. 2.6

Explanation: You can use internal JSON libraries in 2.6. Older Python versions use a library named simplejson.

2. What is the first line of code you need to write to use JSON functions within your Python scripts?

import json

Explanation: You much import the JSON library to use its functions. If you attempt to use JSON functions without first importing this library, your code will throw an error.

3. What is the Python function that turns a Python string into a JSON object?

a. loads
b. port
c. import
d. convert

Explanation: The loads function takes a string that you've set up in your Python code and turns it into a JSON object where you can retrieve values based on the JSON structural variables. The string can come from a database or another Python script or even user input.

4. Write the Python class sample we created with the customer first and last name as the two properties for the class.

```
class Customer(object):
    def __init__(self, firstname, lastname):
        self.firstname = firstname
        self.lastname = lastname
user = Customer ('John', 'Smith')
```

Explanation: This customer object can be converted to a JSON object.

5. What is the term given to converting a class object to a JSON string object?

a. serialization
b. conversion

c. transforming

d. changing

Explanation: Serialization is the process of turning an object to a flat string that you can use to print the values to your user's screen.

Chapter 10: JSON in C#

Objective: C# is the language for web applications and Windows desktops. This chapter shows you how to work with C# and JSON objects.

If you want to create web applications that run on Windows servers, you'll need to know the C# language. C# is one of the most popular backend coding languages on the Internet. It's a more difficult language to learn because it focuses on object oriented coding structures, but it's a robust language that offers several options for web programmers. One option is using it with JSON. C# has its own libraries for working with C#.

An Introduction to C#

This eBook isn't about C#, but it's good to know the language and its background before you jump into it and start using JSON collaboratively.

C# is a part of the ASP.NET language framework. ASP.NET is a group of libraries, and you use either C# or VB.NET to work with these libraries. VB.NET didn't take off like C#, so most coders use C# as the backend technology for web applications. C# was originally introduced with the .NET framework in 2002 with the new Visual Studio released by Microsoft.

When you work with C#, you'll need to have a strong grasp of object oriented programming (OOP), which makes it one of the more difficult languages to learn.

OOP is a great way to build large applications. OOP has the concept of creating code around compartments. Each section of the application is created in a class. For instance, if you are writing code for a car, you would create a class for the car's engine, the interior, the trunk, the transmission and the exterior. These classes are put together to form the car or application.

If you recall from the previous two chapters, we also used classes in PHP and Python and transferred them to JSON objects. You can do the same in C#, but C# usually works hand in hand with Ajax to make calls back and forth between web pages. C# is a backend language, so you use it with several API applications. You might even use C# to create your own API. When you create your own API, your users will expect you to send them JSON format. You might be asked to use XML as well, but most developers use the JSON syntax and will expect it when they work with your API services.

C# is a very popular web application programming language, so we'll focus this chapter on a web application setup. Just remember that you can use C# for desktop applications as well. Since we're focusing on web applications, we'll need to use HTML and Ajax for our C# code.

You'll also need Visual Studio to carry out any C# programming even though JSON is a simple text format. Visual Studio contains the compiler used to put the files together and turn them into binary applications. You then upload these binary files to the web server, which can use them to display your web pages.

One thing to note is that C# is very platform dependent. It only works on a Windows web server, so you'll need Windows hosting and a Windows developer environment to work with the language. Visual Studio has a great way to interface and integrate into the Windows server environment. The Windows server environment uses Internet Information Services (IIS) to host web pages. You can't run the Windows binaries on another type of web host such as Linux. You'll need this information when you determine the structure for your web application and where you want to host them.

One last thing to note in C#. Microsoft has moved towards an MVC type architecture. MVC stands for model, view and controller. The URLs used in the MVC architecture are much different than what you'd expect if you are a PHP coder. MVC changes the URLs dependent on the controller name. There is no file extension that shows in an MVC URL. This can be confusing to some coders who are just starting out with C#.

MVC works with the idea that each component of an application is separated into a controller, a model and a view. The controller in C# is the business logic of the application. It contains much of the C# code that you need to know. The model is the container for the data and information you pass back and forth between your applications. Models are closely used with the database and any data you pass back and forth between your applications. The view is the actual web page that displays the information you've retrieved from the controller and model.

Getting Started

Now that you know a little bit of background for C#, you can now get started with a test application to work with C# and JSON.

We mentioned that you need Visual Studio to code with C#. In previous chapters we discussed Notepad+, but with this specific chapter you'll need the Visual Studio working environment. It takes several minutes for Visual Studio to install on your machine, so take plenty of time to set up your work environment when you decide to code in C#

First, we need our web page. Let's take the code from the previous chapters and use it with our C# application.

```html
<!DOCTYPE html>
<html>
<head>
<script src="jquery-1.11.3.min.js"></script>
</head>
<body>

<h2>JSON User Account Example</h2>

<p id="myuser"></p>

<script>
$(document).ready(function () {
$.getJSON('http://mydomain.com/json', {
user_account_id: '100' }, function(data) {
    var user = data
            var firstname = user.FirstName;
            var lastname = user.LastName;
            var accounted = user.AccountId;
            var output = "First Name: " + firstname
+ "<br>" +
                "Last Name: " + lastname + "<br>"
+
                "Account Id: " + accounted;
            $('#myuser').html(output);
});
```

```
});
</script>

</body>
</html>
```

You'll notice that we changed only one piece of code from the previous chapter. We change the target URL where the JSON is parsed. When you work with the MVC pattern in C#, the framework changes URLs to match the name of the controller. In this example, we're using the JSON controller, so the URL and target URL from the Ajax function is the json notation.

You place this code in your view that you create in Visual Studio. Note that Visual Studio uses a much different format than a regular HTML file, so you'll need to add this to the CSHTML file that you create when you create your application solution and the controller. Visual Studio creates a default CSHTML file and controller called "Home" when you create your project, so you can use this file instead of making a new one. The main different between a CSHTML file and a regular HTML file is that the Visual Studio view can use a programming language named Razor. This language lets you call C# code within the file instead of using HTML. It includes library helper functions and a way to connect your view with a model. All of these features can be learned while you're learning the C# language.

After you copy and paste the above code into your Visual Studio view file, it's time to work with your controller. The controller is what takes the input from the Ajax call, manipulates the JSON data that you sent it, and then display it for your users.

You first want to create a variable for the input. In this example, we're using the accountId variable to do a lookup for a customer. You need to first create an accountId variable for the customer.

Next, we need a Dictionary object. This lesson isn't about C#, so we won't go into a Dictionary class object. Dictionary objects hold key-value pairs that you can use within your C# codes. They are an efficient way to work with JSON or other key-value pairs that you don't know what the values should be. You store the values in the dictionary object and then pass it back to the calling page, which in this case is the Visual Studio view you set up earlier.

Let's take a look at what creating a dictionary object looks like in C#.

```
Dictionary<string, string> customer = new Dictionary<string, string>();
```

The above code is a dictionary object with the name given as customer. This is the way you instantiate the object in C#. You'll see this type of coding in any C# application you work with.

Now you want to take your user input that you take from the Ajax submission. Since we have an account ID, we want to add an account ID to the dictionary object. Let's take a look at the code.

```
var accountId = inputAccountId; //this is the input variable
```
we get from the MVC controller when it receives input from your Ajax view code that we displayed earlier.
```
Dictionary<string, string> customer = new Dictionary<string, string>();
customer.Add("accountId", accountId);
```

We added the accountId variable and kept the dictionary instantiation code. But, let's take a closer look at the third line of code which is important when we're working with Ajax and JSON.

Look at the customer object and the addition of the key-value pair using the Add function. The Add method on the dictionary object is used to put a new key-value pair in the object. In this case, we've created a key-value pair for the customer's accountId. Note that the first parameter in the list is the string accountId. This accountId is not the actual variable value. It's the key part of the key-value pair that indicates to the C# compiler that you're giving this key-value pair the name accountId.

The second parameter is the actual account ID that you want to store in the key-value pair. This value is from the page input in the Ajax and HTML code. You want to set it in the dictionary object to store it for later use.

Now it's time to convert the dictionary object to a JSON object string. Luckily, the C# language has its own libraries that let you do it without much effort. This library is a part of the C# and ASP.NET framework, so you don't need to download any special programs, dlls or any other external program for your local application solution.

Let's take a look at the new code.

```
var accountId = inputAccountId; //this is the input variable
we get from the MVC controller when it receives input from
your Ajax view code that we displayed earlier.
Dictionary<string, string> customer = new Dictionary<string,
string>();
customer.Add("accountId", accountId);
string js = JsonConvert.SerializeObject(customer);
```

Notice that we created a string object. It's important to remember that with C# you have primitive strings and class strings. This is a primitive string, which is the standard data type for a C# application that requires character input. A string class is actually a class and has much more options to manipulate any string input. We just want to work with a standard string variable, which is what we have defined.

The important part of this line of code is the JsonConvert class and its associated SerializeObject method. You know that the JsonConvert part of the statement is a class because it's separated with a dot and then the method is used to actually perform the action on the JSON object. The SerializeObject method is a part of the class, and it's the method that actually does the action on the JSON object. It converts it to a flat string that you can then use in your HTML page that we created earlier. You can also print the result to the screen to view the string. The following code shows you how to display the output to the string.

```
var accountId = inputAccountId; //this is the input variable
we get from the MVC controller when it receives input from
your Ajax view code that we displayed earlier.
Dictionary<string, string> customer = new Dictionary<string,
string>();
customer.Add("accountId", accountId);
string js = JsonConvert.SerializeObject(customer);
System.Diagnostics.Debug.WriteLine(js);
```

We added just one more line of code to this block of code. We write the js variable to the debug window, which you will find at the bottom of your Visual Studio environment. This is the way you debug strings and objects while you program yoru C# applications.

While the debug line of code displays the information to the debugger, you still need to return the object to the Ajax calling function so that it can display the information to the user. You just use the return statement to return content back to the user. Let's see what this line of code would look like in your Visual Studio solution.

```
var accountId = inputAccountId; //this is the input variable
we get from the MVC controller when it receives input from
your Ajax view code that we displayed earlier.
Dictionary<string, string> customer = new Dictionary<string,
string>();
customer.Add("accountId", accountId);
string js = JsonConvert.SerializeObject(customer);
System.Diagnostics.Debug.WriteLine(js);
return js;
```

The return statement returns the JSON object back to the controller that called the function. Let's take a look at the HTML page again with the Ajax call.

```
<!DOCTYPE html>
<html>
<head>
<script src="jquery-1.11.3.min.js"></script>
</head>
<body>

<h2>JSON User Account Example</h2>

<p id="myuser"></p>

<script>
$(document).ready(function () {
$.getJSON('http://mydomain.com/json', {
user_account_id: '100' }, function(data) {
    var user = data
```

```
            var firstname = user.FirstName;
            var lastname = user.LastName;
            var accounted = user.AccountId;
            var output = "First Name: " + firstname
+ "<br>" +
                "Last Name: " + lastname + "<br>"
+
                "Account Id: " + accounted;
            $('#myuser').html(output);
});
});
</script>

</body>
</html>
```

Notice that HTML output. This is the part of the code that displays the data to the user. This is what gives your C# code the ability to send and receive and display the data from your JSON objects.

C# is a much more advanced language, but you can use it to create advanced JSON objects that then can be used in your web applications. Remember that these functions aren't limited to just web applications. You can also make them a part of your APIs or Windows desktop applications when you work with JSON.

Lab Questions

1. What is the JSON class that converts JSON objects in your C# code?

a. JsonConvert
b. Json
c. JsonLibrary
d. JsonInclude

Explanation: The JsonConvert class has several functions and methods that can be used to encode and decode Json objects in your C# code.

2. What is the other language in the ASP.NET framework that you can use to work with web applications using JSON?

a. C++
b. VB.NET
c. Java
d. PHP

Explanation: The ASP.NET framework contains the C# and VB.NET languages that you can use to build web applications that use the JSON data structures.

3. What class object should you use to create a JSON object that is later sent to the calling CSHTML view in C#?

a. Dictionary
b. List
c. Java
d. Array

Explanation: The Dictionary class makes it easy to create key-value pairs that you can use to then send data back and forth in your frontend pages.

Conclusion

This book has found you because you have the ultimate potential.

It may be easy to think and feel that you are limited but the truth is you are more than what you have assumed you are. We have been there. We have been in such a situation: when giving up or settling with what is comfortable feels like the best choice. Luckily, the heart which is the dwelling place for passion has told us otherwise.

It was in 2014 when our team was created. Our compass was this – the dream of coming up with books that can spread knowledge and education about programming. The goal was to reach as many people across the world. For them to learn how to program and in the process, find solutions, perform mathematical calculations, show graphics and images, process and store data and much more. Our whole journey to make such dream come true has been very pivotal in our individual lives. We believe that a dream shared becomes a reality.

We want you to be part of this journey, of this wonderful reality. We want to make learning programming easy and fun for you. In addition, we want to open your eyes to the truth that programming can be a start-off point for more beautiful things in your life.

Programming may have this usual stereotype of being too geeky and too stressful. We would like to tell you that nowadays, we enjoy this lifestyle: surf-program-read-write-eat.

How amazing is that? If you enjoy this kind of life, we assure you that nothing is impossible and that like us, you can also make programming a stepping stone to unlock your potential to solve problems, maximize solutions, and enjoy the life that you truly deserve.

This book has found you because you are at the brink of everything fantastic!

Thanks for reading!

<u>You can be interested in:</u>
"Javascript: *Learn Javascript In A DAY!*"

Here is our full library: http://amzn.to/1HPABQI

To your success,
Acodemy.

Made in the USA
San Bernardino, CA
23 July 2016